Children in Crisis

Violence, Victims, and Victories

Marcel Lebrun

ROWMAN & LITTLEFIELD EDUCATION

A division of

ROWMAN & LITTLEFIELD PUBLISHERS, INC.
Lanham • New York • Toronto • Plymouth, UK

Published by Rowman & Littlefield Education
A division of Rowman & Littlefield Publishers, Inc.
A wholly owned subsidiary of The Rowman & Littlefield Publishing Group, Inc.
4501 Forbes Boulevard, Suite 200, Lanham, Maryland 20706
http://www.rowmaneducation.com

Estover Road, Plymouth PL6 7PY, United Kingdom

British Library Cataloguing in Publication Information Available

Library of Congress Cataloging-in-Publication Data

Lebrun, Marcel, 1957–
  Children in crisis : violence, victims, and victories / Marcel Lebrun.
   p. cm.
  Includes bibliographical references and index.
  ISBN 978-1-61048-020-8 (cloth : alk. paper) — ISBN 978-1-61048-021-5 (pbk. : alk. paper) — ISBN 978-1-61048-022-2 (electronic)
  1. Children and violence—United States.   2. School violence—United States.
3. Violence in children—United States.   4. Children and violence—United States—Prevention.   5. School violence—United States—Prevention.   6. Violence in children—United States—Prevention.   I. Title.
  HQ784.V55L43   2011
  303.6083'0973—dc23   2011026285

Printed in the United States of America

Children in Crisis

Violence, Victims, and Victories

Dedication

I dedicate this book to all the children in the world who do not have a chance to be successful because life has dealt them a series of situations or events that is beyond their control. Childhood is something that is precious and can never be regained. It is our duty to provide a safe passage to all children as they grow.

Table of Contents

Foreword

What is more important than our children? As parents, educators, care providers, and citizens, our first priority is to raise the next generation to be safe, healthy, and intelligent contributors to society. However, to successfully accomplish this enormous task, we must pay extra-special attention to those children who are in crisis—those who have been victims of violence, have forms of psychopathology, are sex offenders or victims of sex offences, are substance abusers or involved in the foster, juvenile detention, or prison systems. Marcel Lebrun's well-written and researched book covers these important topics and more, including personal, national, and international perspectives. All people who work with or care about children should be aware of the topics in these pages as we must work together to save children in crisis. As we know, it "takes a village" to raise a child. To raise a child in crisis it takes our global village working together. This book goes beyond the local and national perspectives and examines global perspectives as well.

To be able to work effectively together to improve the lives of these children, we must be educated on the topics that Dr. Lebrun has astutely chosen to include in this book. A powerful tool, this book will not only help readers become more knowledgeable about these essential topics but will also provide insights into strategies to improve the lives of all children. We must start with our neediest children to have the greatest impact on all children. This book helps us do that.

Our guide on this journey to improve our understanding of children in crisis and how to best help them is Dr. Marcel Lebrun. He is an award-winning educator and international expert and renowned author with decades of experience working and writing in this area. As a reader, you are in the best possible hands as you take the journey through the pages of this book to better understand this difficult topic.

Kimberly Williams, PhD

Preface

To be a child in the twenty-first century is both a blessing and a curse. These children are faced with new challenges that will be with them for the rest of their lives. They are faced with a variety of critical issues that are inherited from their parents, families, and communities. Millions of children in this country, as well as worldwide, lack safe homes, food to eat, quality childcare, and safe, protective communities to live in. Their lack of proper emotional, psychological, and social modeling has created a generation of individuals which research says will live longer than their parents.

In this century we have better ways to eat, live, and be productive, yet we are losing a generation of children due to a lack of family values, bonding, and nurturance. Instead, we are creating a massive group of children and juveniles who do not have the coping mechanisms to communicate, interact appropriately, or solve problems in a constructive and proactive way.

Since the turn of the century, we have seen an increase in runaways, prostitution, sexual offenders, violent crimes, homelessness, and vehicular accidents for juveniles. A similar increase has also been seen in the use of guns and weapons, school shootings, bullying and victims, and poverty. As you read the rest of this book, you will see that the statistics are staggering, yet there is hope.

In one of the wealthiest countries in the world we have a subculture that exists within our communities. It is one full of subversive, dysfunctional individuals who are only trying to find a place to survive. Often thrown into a life of survival at an early age and with a lack of knowledge, education, or support systems, they create ways they believe will enable them to attain what they believe they deserve, are entitled to, or will allow them to survive another day and not die.

Our society has coined the terms "latchkey kids," "throw away kids," and "garbage kids." Imagine knowing as a child that this is how society sees you. It brings forth a variety of emotions and rage. We often wonder why children act out against mainstream society. I believe it is obvious. We treat these children as lesser than we are, take away their ability to be productive, and enclose them in lock-up facilities, while never reaffirming to them that they are worthwhile individuals. It is a proven fact that once a child-juvenile has embarked on a life of violence it is very difficult to change or be rehabilitated. The end result for many of these juveniles is early death or a life of incarceration. Not a great choice, in my opinion.

This book will reveal to you the inner workings of each type of behavior disorder kid, as well as the motivations behind behaviors. It is my belief that most children are not born dysfunctional, but they are created by the people in their lives and in the society they see as a role model. The way to change a life is to be part of it, to be involved, to remain consistent, and to stay informed and connected in as many ways as possible, even during the tough times. It is even more crucial to stay involved during the crises, or difficult events that individuals face on a daily basis. It is a known fact that if children feel valued they are less likely to act out or resort to violence and other such means to get their needs met.

By being present, we communicate that we are there to protect, educate, support, reinforce, and guide. The challenge will be to do this consistently for all children that come into our midst. Our mission is that no child is left out, thrown away, or abandoned because of their behavior. Every child has a right to be successful—it is our duty as educators, parents, caregivers, government officials, and citizens to make sure that every child gets the chance they deserve.

Acknowledgments

I would like to thank my graduate assistants Megan Brown and Ashley Borthwick-Mosson for their assistance in doing some of the research.

I wish to thank all of my family and friends for their support over the years, you believing in me encouraged me to continue to reach new heights.

Chapter 1

The Scope of the Problem

Children living in the twenty-first century face many critical issues. These issues are not new and have remained fairly consistent throughout the decades. It seems ironic that we have become more technologically savvy and efficient in our everyday lives, yet we still have many children who are casualties of this new technological age.

We still have many poor, undernourished, neglected, abused, and violent teenagers and children who succeed in achieving an early death or incarceration. A sad fact is that many states are able to predict with a good level of accuracy how many prison beds they will need ten years down the road based on school standardized tests and number of students at-risk or receiving specialized services in elementary school.

There are approximately 74 million children in the United States of America. "A child is born into poverty every 33 seconds. A child is abused or neglected every 35 seconds. A child is born uninsured every 39 seconds. A child dies before his or her first birthday every 18 minutes. A child or teen is killed by gunfire every 3 hours" (Children's Defense Fund, November 2009). Why the chaos? Why are the children of America in such crisis?

Statistics are wake-up calls for politicians and a society as a whole. The following were reported by the Children's Defense Fund (2009): Almost 1 in 13 children in the United States—5.8 million—lives in extreme poverty. In 2008, a family of four was classified as extremely poor if its household income was below $10,600, or half of the official poverty line. Young children are more likely than school-age children to live in extreme poverty.

More than half of all poor children in the United States live in eight states: California, Texas, New York, Florida, Illinois, Ohio, Georgia, and Michigan. The child poverty rate was 18.2 percent as of January 2010.

1

There are more poor White, non-Hispanic children than Black children. However, Hispanic and Black children are about three times more likely to live in poverty than White or non-Hispanic children. Children who live in inner cities, rural areas, the South, or in female-headed families are more likely to be poor (Children's Defense Fund 2009).

Children under age six are more likely to be poor than school-age children. Poverty and race are the primary factors underpinning the pipeline to prison. In fact, Black juveniles are about four times as likely as their White peers to end up being incarcerated.

The number of poor children was at its lowest in 1973. Since 2000, both the number and the rate have risen. There are now 13.3 million poor children in the United States, an increase of 500,000 between 2008 and 2009. These numbers are expected to increase as families face the full impact of the recession.

The child poverty rate dropped substantially in the 1960s, then rose significantly in the early 1980s. Great strides were made in decreasing child poverty in the late 1990s, owing in part to the strong economy. However, the child poverty rate was higher in 2009 than at the beginning of the decade. Child poverty is closely tied to the overall health of the economy, rising in periods of recession.

More than 14 million children in America are poor, but they live in working families. Research in education has proven that children who live in poverty are more likely to lag behind their peers, are less healthy, trail in emotional and intellectual development, and are less likely to graduate from high school. The extremely sad statistic is that the cycle will remain unbroken and they will become parents saddled with poverty. Keeping children in poverty costs a half-trillion dollars in lost productivity, poorer health, and increased crime. To end child poverty, there has to be investment in quality education, livable wages for families, child care support, and health coverage.

Oftentimes poverty comes with violence. There are many unintentional firearm injuries occurring throughout the United States. Unintentional shootings account for nearly 20 percent of all firearm-related fatalities among children ages 14 and under, compared with 3 percent for the entire U.S. population. The unintentional firearm injury death rate among children ages 14 and under in the United States is 9 times higher than in 25 other industrialized countries combined.

There are actions that can be taken to protect children from gun violence. We as a nation can begin to support common-sense gun safety measures. There has to be a more stringent enforcement of gun laws at the state and federal levels. Americans have to cease their fascination with guns. Firearms must be removed from homes where children are present. Guns don't kill; people do. We need to stress nonviolent values and conflict resolution.

Children have to see that solving problems occurs through communication, not the use of force and bullets.

Our media is bombarded with images of guns, violence, and aggression. Many advocates of gun control also embark on campaigns to refuse to buy or use products that glamorize violence. How many video games are out there where your success as a player depends on how many people you can kill? Do we intentionally give children the subconscious message that you are a winner if you destroy all your adversaries?

Children and teens need alternative models on which to base their values. We as a society need to provide safe zones, both inside the house and outside in the community. Are we capable of changing a whole culture that is based in violence? If we look elsewhere in the world violence to this proportion is not present.

"Approximately one-third of families with children representing more than 22 million children in 11 million homes, keep at least one gun in the house. Nearly all childhood unintentional shooting deaths occur in and or, around the home. Fifty percent occur in the home of the victim, and nearly 40 percent occur in the home of a friend or relative. The gun of choice is a handgun. Unintentional shootings seem to occur outside of school when children are unsupervised (4–5 pm, weekends, summer months, and holidays)" (www. preventinjury.com).

Staggering statistics from the Children's Defense Fund indicate that "the number of children killed by guns in 2006 would fill more than 127 public school classrooms of 25 students each. More preschoolers were killed by firearms than law enforcement officers killed in the line of duty. Since 1979, gun violence has ended the lives of 107,603 children and teens in America." The sad part about this is that these numbers continue to rise every year— when will it stop?

One in three Black boys and one in six Latino boys born in 2001 are at risk of going to prison in their lifetime. Boys are five times more likely to go to prison than girls; however, the number of girls in the juvenile system is on the rise dramatically. We have to begin changing our education system so that children and teenagers do not enter the pipeline to prison or early death. How will we do this?

We can begin by treating youths at risk as potentially productive members of society instead of lost causes in prison cages. We need to empower children to have a vision of their future and the role they play in those goals being attained. Everyone in America needs to have the possibility of being successful, productive, and happy.

It is essential that communities begin establishing community-based alternatives to detention. Youths at risk need to be looked at individually and receive individualized and developmentally appropriate services and direction. There has to be better collaboration between all the agencies who service this population. Improving collaboration with mental health agencies, as well as child welfare systems, juvenile justice systems, and education professionals, would go a long way in improving these long-standing problems.

The system of care needs to be ongoing and to follow up with these youths so that once they are back on the streets they can function as productive members of society and not become a returning visitor to the juvenile correction system.

M. Rosenbach indicated in her 2001 report of the State Children's Health Insurance Program that there were 9–10 million uninsured children in America. The numbers have now increased so that there are more like 12–13 million children without insurance. "Every 39 seconds a child is born uninsured, meaning that more than 2200 children are born every day uninsured. The number of children enrolled in the State Children's Health Insurance Program is approximately 7 million. There are over 32 million children enrolled in Medicaid. Child enrollment accounts for over 49% of all people enrolled in Medicaid, yet medical expenditures for children only account for about 22% of total Medicaid expenditures." Our health care system is in crisis.

The present system is extremely complicated, very expensive, and often unattainable to families who are barely surviving in their daily lives. Our challenge is to get health care to those who need it the most. Can we really afford to have a whole generation of children and teenagers who are not receiving adequate health care? Congress has made a movement toward universal health care; however, there is still a long way to go so that the children of this country will be properly served and taken care of in a meaningful way.

Education in the United States is also in crisis. School districts do not have the money to adequately fund programs, salaries, and services. The amount spent per pupil in public schools is around $8 thousand per student. This amount varies according to state. The percent of public school fourth graders performing below grade level in reading is about 68 percent nationwide, and in math, it is 61 percent.

Why are our schools failing? What do we need to do to infuse a layer of professionalism and success? Is it by better teacher education programs at the higher education institutions? Is it by dumping in more money? Is it time to overhaul the system as it stands? Why is the rest of the world progressing while America, which is often seen as a leader in education, is falling behind or invested in keeping the status quo?

We have become better aware of how children learn, how they develop, how the brain works, and how to improve methodology, and yet our school systems remain in crisis. What needs to be done? Is it time to become completely individual student–directed and abandon the system as it now exists? The investigation and data collection needs to continue; however, we need to stop ignoring the problems and move toward change and solutions that will revolutionize how we do business in our public schools.

The child welfare system is also in chaos in this country. The number of children who are victims of abuse and neglect tops over 900,000 (U.S. Department of Commerce, 2008). "If we break down the abuse by category, Neglect and Medical Neglect account for 73 percent of all cases. Physical Abuse is about 16 percent, and Sexual Abuse is 9.5–10 percent. Psychological and other maltreatment is about 15 percent" (National Data on Child Abuse, 2007).

"The number of children in foster care is over 500,000. Their average length of stay in foster care is about 27.2 months" (www.adoptionlearning-partners.org/foster_to_forever.cfm). Research indicates that if a child or youth is in two or fewer placements, the likelihood of them remaining there less than 12 months is about 84 percent. The more placements the child or youth has, the odds that the placements will be longer and more than 24 months is about 32 percent. These numbers are staggering. Why are there so many children in crisis?

The reasons are that their parents and their communities are in crisis. Adults can barely look after themselves, and yet they are charged with looking after their children. Many do not have the capacity or the means to be parents but obviously do become parents.

The number of grandparents raising their grandchildren is almost 3 million individuals. This is becoming part of the national norm. In the past, it was rare to see grandparents becoming the primary caretakers, but now in some communities it is a very normal and accepted part of life. Grandparents, instead of looking forward to retirement, are now being asked to raise a second family, in many circumstances without adequate financial means.

"Of the many children who end up in foster care (500,000), only about 50,000 ever get adopted permanently into a home, so where do the others go?" (yourbloodismyblood.blogspot.com). Who looks after them? How many of these 500,000 end up in our jails and in the streets?

Youths at risk in the United States do not graduate from high school. The national dropout rate is anywhere from 6.7 percent to 30 percent in some communities. Youths who do not graduate from high school also have a 15–20 percent unemployment rate. There the environment is ripe for crime. The number of juvenile arrests last year in this country was almost 1.3 million youths (School system.org).

These youths end up in either jail or residential facilities and account for huge tax burdens on certain states and communities. It is almost 2.8 times more expensive to keep a youth in jail then it is to keep them in school. If we look at the situation from a financial point of view we know we need to keep them going to school until they can graduate and find employment. The one way to do so is to revamp what youths learn and do in high schools. The high schools of America need to become more progressive and to match the needs of their clients.

Now that I have completely demoralized and depressed you in these first few pages, it is important to remember that we are not helpless; we can effect change. We can begin by protecting children. We can educate parents. We can empower teachers. We can motivate lawmakers and politicians. We can begin one child at a time.

Chapter 2

Violence in the Schools

School violence is unacceptable, yet it happens every single day in America. Why has violence become such a part of our culture? Violence is now tolerated in most communities and schools. We talk about regaining the power to provide safe schools, yet we have bullying statistics that are out of proportion, attacks on teachers are up, students are being caught for having weapons at school, and children and youth are using violence as a way to solve problems or communicate their frustration with the existing school system.

"In a nationwide survey of high school students, about 6% reported not going to school on one or more days in the 30 days preceding the survey because they felt unsafe, either at school or on their way to and from school" (CDC 2010). It is unfathomable that youths do not feel safe in the one place that they should always be taken care of by adults.

"Nearly 700,000 young people ages 10 to 24 are treated in emergency departments each year, for injuries sustained due to violence-related assaults" (CDC 2009). If there are so many attacks every year, why are school officials not putting in resources or support to protect students?

"On average, 16 persons between the ages of 10 and 24 are murdered each day in the United States" (CDC 2009). This number of victims is horrendous. A life wasted, a potential never realized.

"In addition to causing injury and death, youth violence affects communities by increasing the cost of health care, reducing productivity, decreasing property values, and disrupting social services" (Mercy et al. 2002). Society as a whole needs to make sure that violence is addressed immediately and effectively, as the costs to intervene after the fact are way too high.

"Juveniles accounted for 16% of all violent crime arrests and 26% of all property crime arrests in 2008. In 2008, 1,280 juveniles were arrested

7

for murder, 3,340 for forcible rape, and 56,000 for aggravated assault" (Puzzanchera 2009).

In a 2009 nationally representative sample of youth in grades 9–12:

- 11.1 percent reported being in a physical fight on school property
- 15.1 percent of male students and 6.7 percent of female students reported being in a physical fight on school property
- 5.0 percent did not go to school on one or more days because they felt unsafe, either at school or on their way to or from school.
- 5.6 percent reported carrying a weapon (gun, knife, or club) on school property, on one or more days
- 7.7 percent reported being threatened or injured with a weapon on school property, one or more times (CDC 2010b).

Educators know that prevention is the key. Programs to teach new skills will lead to better problem-solving and social skills; however, it does not seem to be enough. Awareness, knowledge, and better communication are known to address school violence, yet we seem to act too late or not at all in many circumstances.

If we step back into history we sometimes idealize the past—a past that was tranquil and safe. However, schools in the 50s and 60s were rife with violence. Integration was occurring, the public school system served many children living in large urban centers who lived in poverty, and violence was present on the streets. If one looks at these communities, school was still one of the safest places.

Schools in the past generally ran organizational structures and policies as a way of protecting the students and faculty. Children and youth were supervised and monitored by many trained professionals and therefore were often guided to make better choices in their behaviors. Part of growing up is making mistakes; however, it was encouraged back then to make choices that were aligned with what society thought was appropriate. Children received in many instances very specific role modeling to be able to be functioning citizens in the future and to have a very clear set or code of values and morals.

The need for better prepared educational professionals is a challenge. Higher education institutions need to be able to empower future and existing administrators with strategies and knowledge that will make them effective in dealing with troubled youths and their behaviors. It is a well-known fact that many educators do not intervene when they see problem behaviors because of a fear for their personal safety. These educators, by being fearful, are contributing to the power that these youths may have in controlling the situation. Is a trained policeman the solution to school violence and behavior intervention?

Educators will often report that their job is to teach, and I would agree 100 percent with that statement; however, to teach means to discipline as well. If a child or youth is unable to meet the expectations of a classroom or a school, then that child needs to be taught replacement behaviors that will enable him or her to meet those expectations. It is only by teaching new coping and problem-solving skills that we can get children and youth to make different choices, rather than using violence as a way to attain or meet their needs.

In education we see a trend toward arming schools with metal detectors. The state of New York, in 2009, spent $28 million to add security to schools. Do these metal detectors make the school safer, or is the fact that there are now adults monitoring the students making the schools safer? I would suppose that the two actions together make a school safer. However, it is such a small intervention in the full course of actions. Students and faculty both need to be taught new ways of behaving and coping with the daily stress of school.

Schools are violent in the United States but relatively safe places in other parts of the world. Why is there more violence in America than anywhere else? What are we doing differently or wrong? What are European schools doing well? The answers I believe are embedded in the culture. American culture has a very egocentric base, and the rights of the individual are the prime focus. In other cultures, you are an individual within a social group, whether it is family or community. Your rights do not supersede all the rights of others. Can we help American children become more socialistic in their thinking and actions, or is it already too late for this generation and the next?

Children and youth in America will often be identified early on in the school system as having behavioral challenges, some as early as three years old. I have personally worked with children as young as three years old who have been expelled from preschool. The deviant or oppositional behaviors present themselves early. These children come into the school system already challenged by their early years' experiences, and often their pathology is already being rooted in their personalities. Psychologists, counselors, and special education teachers are mobilized into action to prepare behavior support plans and individual education plans.

Early on it is not difficult to identify the factors that lead to these types of behavioral issues. Educators are often quick to blame parents as the root cause. Ineffective parental guidelines and rules have created this little monster in kindergarten. We need to get beyond the fact that the responsibility lies solely with the parents. As educators, we need to teach the skill set that is missing in the repertoire of this problem student.

Research on youth violence has increased our understanding of factors that make some populations more vulnerable to victimization and perpetration. Risk factors increase the likelihood that a young person will become violent.

"Risk factors are not direct causes of youth violence; instead, risk factors contribute to youth violence" (Mercy et al. 2002; DHHS 2001). It is important to factor in that times are different, children's behaviors and the family structures are not consistent in all communities, and that expectations are not often enforced or valued.

A number of factors can increase the risk of a youth engaging in violence, but the presence of these factors does not always mean that a young person will become an offender. Research associates the following risk factors with perpetration of youth violence (DHHS 2001; Lipsey and Derzon 1998; Resnick et al. 2004):

- Prior history of violence
- Drug, alcohol, or tobacco use
- Association with delinquent peers
- Poor family functioning
- Poor grades in school
- Poverty in the community

Individual Risk Factors

- History of violent victimization
- Attention deficits, hyperactivity, or learning disorders
- History of early aggressive behavior
- Involvement with drugs, alcohol, or tobacco
- Low IQ
- Poor behavioral control
- Deficits in social cognitive or information-processing abilities
- High emotional distress
- History of treatment for emotional problems
- Antisocial beliefs and attitudes
- Exposure to violence and conflict in the family

Family Risk Factors

- Authoritarian childrearing attitudes
- Harsh, lax, or inconsistent disciplinary practices
- Low parental involvement
- Low emotional attachment to parents or caregivers
- Low parental education and income
- Parental substance abuse or criminality
- Poor family functioning
- Poor monitoring and supervision of children

Peer and Social Risk Factors

- Association with delinquent peers
- Involvement in gangs
- Social rejection by peers
- Lack of involvement in conventional activities
- Poor academic performance
- Low commitment to school and school failure

Community Risk Factors

- Diminished economic opportunities
- High concentrations of poor residents
- High level of transiency
- High level of family disruption
- Low levels of community participation
- Socially disorganized neighborhood

Whenever a list of criteria is developed, one must always add an additional caution. It often will depend on the individual child or youth. These criteria are meant to begin the discussion and not meant to diagnose. They are excellent indicators that may begin the conversation or direct the assessment of each individual case. There is no magic number of risk factors that will lead to any certainty of predictability to being involved in violence of any type.

Protective Factors for the Perpetration of Youth Violence

Protective factors buffer young people from the risks of becoming violent. These factors exist at various levels. To date, protective factors have not been studied as extensively or rigorously as risk factors. However, identifying and understanding protective factors are equally as important as researching risk factors.

Studies propose the following protective factors (DHHS 2001; Resnick et al. 2004):

Individual and Family Protective Factors

- Intolerant attitude toward deviance
- High IQ
- High grade-point average
- Positive social orientation
- Religiosity

- Connectedness to family or adults outside the family
- Ability to discuss problems with parents
- Perceived parental expectations about school performance are high
- Frequent shared activities with parents
- Consistent presence of parent during at least one of the following: when awakening, when arriving home from school, at evening mealtime, or going to bed
- Involvement in social activities

Peer and Social Protective Factors

- Commitment to school
- Involvement in social activities

An observation of the at-risk factors and the protective factors helps us see very easily that there are more at-risk factors present that will lead to the likeliness of a youth acting out. However, the list for protective factors is much less comprehensive but is very much based on relationships with others. The power of people cannot be underestimated; adults can be a positive factor in prevention.

Accessibility to weapons is another strong component of violence in the schools. Americans seem to love their guns and feel a need to have them close by. However, when you look at the attacks upon teachers and students, it is often not guns that are the primary weapon in assaults. Gun control does prevent some violence, but is not solely the answer.

Another factor is lack of teacher involvement or relationship building with students. I have found that children consistently admire and respect those teachers that are strict in setting high standards for behavior and academic performance, and who demonstrate a personal interest in their students. Most schools have at least one such teacher, but too often that teacher functions in isolation rather than being utilized as a role model. Establishing mentoring relationships among teachers and encouraging collaboration through dialogue over these issues is one way of spreading knowledge and experience around.

School community is another factor that can lead to school violence. If the school is not a place where students feel respected and have a sense of dignity and attachment, then these students will not want to be part of the community and therefore will have learned to cope and survive within that community because the law says that they must be in school. If there is a level of dissatisfaction with the school, the adults, and the type of education students are receiving, then it is more likely there will be violence.

Schools that are based on respect, commitment, empowerment, responsibility, and safety are environments where students want to be and violence is not a major factor. It all seems to be about engagement and acceptance. If students feel a sense of belonging, they are more likely to be involved, on multiple levels, with making the school a safe place.

The problems of urban schools are complicated by their connection to poverty, crime, and despair in the urban environment. Living in these communities is both a hazard and a safety risk. Urban schools are challenged in that they need to address the academic needs of their students, but they must also find the resources, the faculty, and the community agencies to provide social, psychological, behavioral, and emotional support to students and their families. The question is where are these resources available in these tough economic times of budget deficits and shortfalls? Schools are not equipped to deal with all the social issues that have found their way into the schools. So, the question becomes how we can make sure to get the necessary personnel in the right positions, and at the right time, for the student in need.

Effective interventions will depend on schools being able to identify, early on, the issues for students and supporting them in a way that leads to students becoming independent problem solvers and better communicators.

There has been much media attention about student profiling being used as a way to predict whether a student will be predisposed to violence, based on a set criteria of behavior indicators. Can one really accurately predict when, and by whom, violence will occur? The answer is no. Can we absolutely identify red flags of behavior? The FBI's Behavioral Sciences Unit has been instrumental in developing set criteria for identification of serial killers and psychologically impaired criminals and successfully capturing them so that they are not able to inflict the harm that they could have done if left unchecked or free to roam in society.

Based on a series of events it is always easier, in hindsight, to identify the signs of a potentially acting-out child or youth. You will never know if you overreact, but you will always know if you underreact. Should schools become more involved in student profiling and work closely with the skills of the FBI? Will bringing a law monitoring agency into the school system make our schools safer and decrease the violence? Some school districts in America are giving it a try as a way to address the issue of violence in their public schools.

Opponents of this move believe that youths will become stigmatized by labels that will follow them throughout their educational and professional careers. People believe that educators do not have the right psychological training to be good profilers. Is there a chance of mislabeling or misidentifying a child and creating psychological harm from the identification as a possible deviant or violent child? Absolutely. However, does protecting the rights of the masses supersede the right of the one troubled individual?

It is important that educators be given a list of troublesome characteristics to be on the lookout for; however. the sole responsibility should not be on individual teachers, but on school case-management or crisis-intervention teams. As a collaborative group, educators can better assess all the criteria, and once the analysis has been completed, act with interventions.

It is also important to include people like the bus drivers, cafeteria workers, janitorial staff, and additional teachers, who also interact and can provide, at times, some valuable data to confirm or eliminate the emotional responses that often are part of the daily interactions with these troubled students. The process has to become data-based decision making and not based on personal perceptions and interpretations.

Weapons in the school and community are ever present—the key is to be able to identify whether or not the person has a weapon and whether that person's behavior indicates that they may use it. Michael and Chris Dorn produced a checklist of seven indicators that a weapon is being concealed. It is a well-known fact that an aggressor can belong to any race or ethnic group. They can be from a variety of socioeconomic groups and may have a PhD or be a high school dropout. It can be anyone.

Learn to Recognize These Behaviors: Officers and other campus personnel, such as school counselors and faculty members, have learned to identify the specific indicators that a person may be armed. Michael and Chris Dorn have studied extensively the behaviors that may be present, which would most probably indicate that a youth may have a concealed weapon. It should be noted, however, that the following signs do not always indicate the presence of a weapon:

1. Security Check: Gun violators in particular will typically touch and/or adjust the weapons concealed on their bodies numerous times during the day. This may be a gentle- and-difficult-to-observe bump with the elbow, wrist, or hand. On rare occasions, it could be a distinct grasping of the weapon as they adjust it. Violators often make this gesture when getting out of a chair or a car or when walking up a flight of stairs or high curb.
2. Unnatural Gait: Gun violators may walk with an awkward gait. They may fail to bend their knees because they have rifles or shotguns in their pants. They may also walk uncomfortably because they have guns, knives, or other weapons hidden in their boots or shoes causing

discomfort. Again, the total circumstances will indicate the likelihoo
a weapon being present.

For example, an individual with a disability may also not bend the leg
or walk with an unnatural gait, but he or she will likely not appear to be
nervous. You will also not see the rigid line of a rifle running down the
outer pants leg as the person walks or the periodic bulge from the butt of
the gun above the waistband as it moves back and forth.

3. Jacket Sag: When you place a handgun in a jacket pocket, the coat typically hangs lower on the side where the weapon is located. In addition,
you will often see the fabric pulled tight from the weight of the gun,
and the weapon may swing as a violator walks. Often, the outline of the
weapon may be observed in the pocket area. In some cases, the violator
will attempt to hold or pin the weapon if it begins to swing or beat against
their body.

In cases where the violator becomes extremely nervous when approached by an officer, he or she may actually grasp the weapon to keep
it from swinging or put a hand in the pocket. While this is often seen
when people have items other than a weapon in their pocket, it is also
an indicator that is very typical of the gun violator, particularly when
observed with other behaviors described here.

4. Hunchback Stride: When trying to conceal a shotgun, rifle, or submachine gun under a coat while walking, the butt of the weapon will often
cause a noticeable bulge behind the armpit. Additionally, the jacket does
not move naturally because it is supported by the outline of the weapon.
Also, when someone wears a shoulder holster or straps on a sawed-off
rifle, shotgun, or submachine gun under his or her arm, a bulge in front
of or behind the armpit will often be visible.

5. Bulges and the Outline of a Weapon: An alert officer can often spot the
telltale bulge of the weapon or, in some instances, the distinct outline of
a handgun, knife, or brass knuckles in a violator's pocket. This may also
sometimes be observed in a woman's purse, book bag, or other hand
carried item. In some instances, violators wrap a long gun in a blanket
or long jacket.

6. Visible Weapon: Clearly the most reliable of all the indicators is when
the weapon can actually be seen. It is astounding how many times an
armed intruder has entered a facility with a rifle or shotgun protruding
from under his or her jacket, without being observed by staff.

In some cases, the butt of a handgun is visible because it is sticking
out from a back or front pocket. A more common instance is the clip-on
pocketknife that can be observed clipped to a front pocket or in the waistband.

ɔften observed with the edged weapon violator but
ı with gun violators, palming behaviors often indicate
the observer. The knife violator may run the blade of
ɔng the arm or behind the leg to conceal it from frontal
a target is attacked, a violator will also typically have
ʌed on the intended victim (Michael and Chris Dorn,
July 2006).

Parents and children as well as teachers have fears about school violence. How does a parent prepare a child to go to school when fears are present? Almost every child in America has heard or seen the stories about school violence, or school shootings, and has interpreted the information in his or her own unique way. It is a well-known fact that after a school shooting or murder, children experience all kinds of post-traumatic stress disorder behaviors and anxieties that often will prevent a child or youth from attending school for several days or weeks after an incident.

Some children may be openly frightened. Others may fear that it could happen to them. Still others may feel distanced from the possibility of violence in their own lives, while some may be unable to grasp that this really happened to real people. Some may take a protective stance of cynicism and apathy. However children respond, all of them need help and guidance from the adults who care for them.

The solution is to give attention and listen attentively to what these fears are and address them in a way that the child is able to process the information and not be dismissed because of these irrational fears. If the anxiety persists and school attendance refusal begins to occur it may be time to seek out professional help to effectively address these irrational beliefs and fears.

Teen violence is on the rise and ever-so present in our middle and high schools. It can be overly easy to dismiss peer violence as unimportant, typical of that age group, and harmless, even normalized behavior. That would be a mistake. Any child or teenager that is being physically or sexually assaulted, criminally harassed, robbed, or threatened with violence is a harrowing experience for any person no matter what their age group is. Children expect adults to protect them from harm, and not doing so becomes an issue of irresponsibility.

Children can fear going to school or walking in their own neighborhoods. Many children are often overwhelmed with feelings of vulnerability because they are unsure of their surroundings, anxious about meeting the bully, and worried about revictimization if they have been the target of a bully or a gang of kids. Many will feel self-blame because it is "all their fault." These motions can manifest in a variety of ways, including social withdrawal, depression, social anxiety, the inability to concentrate at school, and even aggression through the use of weapons or cyber-bullying.

Children who have been involved in violence have also experienced what is called primary trauma of a violent victimization. This means that they have internalized the aggression and or victimization and this has led to some sort of emotional or psychological impact.

Officials have long recognized a concept called secondary trauma: how coming forward and cooperating with the criminal justice response can be stressful for victims. Victims often see themselves as tattletales or snitches.

Secondary trauma can occur at the police investigation stage, while the case is processed through the court system, and when victims participate in extra-judicial sanctions. The very act of coming forward and putting oneself in a vulnerable position and self-identifying as a victim can be associated with deep feelings of embarrassment, fear of retaliation, a heightened anxiety, and having feelings of regret. Many children and youth often regret telling as they do not see the benefits of telling of the victimization when they are in the middle of it.

We can't help young people if we don't know what happened. Rightly or wrongly, our system of response requires young victims to disclose their experiences to authorities. Why do most young victims decide against this option? The embarrassment, fear of retaliation, aversion to "ratting," a desire to forget and move on, or perhaps even a rapprochement with the person who hurt them may be underlying factors. For some children it is the fear that they may get their loved ones into trouble for abusing them. It is often all about secrets and protecting those secrets.

Sadly, some are resigned to being a perpetual target. They can feel help-less, hopeless, and even unworthy of our assistance. Among the young people, many feared retaliation by the offender and his or her peer group. For others, violent behavior was normal in their homes, schools, or neighborhoods. The past experiences of youths who "told" may be communicated among the peer group as a cautionary tale. They may have heard about other victims who suffered public exposure, repeat victimization, social ostracism, the need to change schools, and waiting months for resolution of the case in court. The act of telling may create as many (or more) problems as it solves.

A report done by the Ontario Victim Services Secretariat published in 2006 states, "Teens Hurting Teens" highlighted the following stressors of telling and not telling. These are the stressors of "NOT TELLING": I would caution the reader that not all these criteria may be present and that some may be more evident than others. This list is not offered as way to evaluate but as a way for educators and service providers to be alert to the fact that some of these behavioral concerns are present in the youth's acting out.

a) Embarrassment about being a "victim," particularly for sexual offences
b) Belief they are to blame or partly to blame or "deserve" what happened
c) Fear of retaliation or reprisal
d) Not wanting reputation as a "rat"
e) Belief police involvement will be ineffective, or even harmful
f) Fear of not being believed
g) Fear of being blamed
h) Belief violence is "normal" or honorable
i) Rapprochement with offender
j) Concern over consequences for the offender
   (Ontario Victim Services Secretariat, 2006)

As one does an analysis of these reasons, they are all based in fear and the "what if" syndrome. Teens run with these beliefs and fears and thus their behavior is influenced or compromised in such a way that they are paralyzed with fear. This leads to taking no action that could be empowering, but rather a passive response and hiding. It is imperative that adults who work with troubled youth be made aware of what kinds of internal stressors that may be happening on a psychological level. The following is a list of concerns that a victim or aggressor may have if they do tell.

These are the Stressors for TELLING:

a) Friends, classmates, teachers, neighbors will learn what happened
b) Family will learn about what happened
c) Case may be reported in the newspaper and other media
d) People may disbelieve or minimize seriousness of youth's experience
e) Youth may be seen as a "rat" by peers, triggering social ostracism or physical retaliation
f) May attend same school with accused as case is processed
g) Testimony in open court is stressful
h) Youth court cases take an average of five to six months to conclude in most cities
i) Victims often disappointed with sentence
   (Lisa Heslop and Corrine Enright, 2006)

A summary of these stressors sees a correlation in that the behaviors or any action taken will be based on fear. Either way the teen spends valuable energy, both physically and intellectually, in trying to avoid any type of confrontation or involvement. It is worrisome that victims of school violence cannot get the

peace they need to regroup, but instead stay in a state of hi
they tell or don't tell. It is a no-win situation for these teena

If the youth of today cannot feel safe in discussing the
schools and communities, how can we as educators protec
schools if we are not overtly aware of the dangers these teens are in on a daily
basis. The whole process of crime to conviction can be as taxing to the victim
as it is for the offender. Today's juvenile justice system is in dire need of
renovation and reconfiguration. The amount of time from arrest to court date
to sentencing maybe as long as seven to ten months. It is clear that a more
efficient system needs to be developed.

School Violence Prevention Checklist

Many of us are wondering what we can do as parents, educators, and students to ensure school safety. The first step is to know what questions to ask about safety at your school. Here is a school violence prevention checklist from the Department of Education. Action Planning Checklist Prevention (www.peace.ca/actionpreven.htm). This list is meant as a way to begin discussions in schools and communities about how to deal with violence. It is not offered as a cure-all for all that ails public schools in America.

What To Look For—Key Characteristics of Responsive and Safe Schools
    Are my school's characteristics responsive to all children?
    What To Look For—Early Warning Signs of Violence
    Has my school taken steps to ensure that all staff, students, and families:
    Understand the principles underlying the identification of early warning signs?
    Know how to identify and respond to imminent warning signs?
    Are able to identify early warning signs?

What To Do—Intervention: Getting Help for Troubled Children
    Does my school:
    Understand the principles underlying intervention?
    Make early intervention available for students at risk of behavioral problems?
    Provide individualized, intensive interventions for students with severe behavior problems? Have school-wide preventive strategies in place that support early intervention?

What To Do—Crisis Response
    Does my school:
    Understand the principles underlying crisis response
    Have a procedure for intervening during a crisis to ensure safety?
    Know how to respond in the aftermath of tragedy?

This checklist is an excellent tool to begin the dialogue between parents, teachers, students, and administrators.

Bullying has become a huge part of school violence. Bullying differs from other forms of aggression in that it entails an imbalance in power. As with aggression and school violence, bullying occurs within a framework that involves bullies, victims, and bystanders, as well as schools, families, and communities. Bullying is not the same as the most common kinds of teasing, peer conflict, and inappropriate behavior. As such, those behaviors should not necessarily be viewed as "bullying."

Testimonial:

"One-and-a-half years ago my now 11-year-old son was threatened with scissors and told he would die in 7 days by a fellow student. I notified the Principal, as well as the Superintendent, of the situation. Nothing was done. Occasional situations have occurred since then but not to the previous scale. This boy has been extremely violent with others to the point of having them removed from the school in a wheel chair. Minor 2-day suspension issued. Now, yesterday he pushed my son and a friend for no reason.

My son's friend retaliated. The boy put his books down in the classroom, came back to where my son and his friend were, and hit the boy who initially hit him. All three boys were given detention. I want to know what course of action I can take if the Principal continues to be so incompetent in providing safety to the kids from this bully. As I stated my son was told he had to serve detention, but I refused as he did nothing wrong. He did not retaliate when pushed and was given the same punishment" (Parent in Minneapolis, MN,; retrieved www.legal-dictionary.thefreedictionary.com/school+violence).

Bullying and aggression occur every single day. This is not an isolated incident, but common throughout schools in America. What should the administrators have done? What is really in their power to do? When does it become a police matter?

Schools should promote a positive school climate that includes school-wide norms of respect and caring and the rejection of bullying. This requires setting clear behavioral expectations for all students in school rules and policies, but also teaching appropriate interpersonal skills for bullies, victims, and bystanders.

The Consortium to Prevent School Bullying has made the following recommendations for schools and school districts to implement as part of their anti-bullying campaign. Permission has been granted by the Consortium to reproduce these recommendations within this text.

SPECIFIC RECOMMENDATIONS

- Develop a comprehensive school-wide plan, to create a positive school climate and norms against bullying, which targets policies, procedures, staff development, and multiple levels of prevention and intervention.
- Emphasize the importance of collaboration and support of the student body, teachers, administrators, parents, and other stakeholders in program development and implementation.
- Use multiple forms of assessment and data to guide decision making. This would include a needs assessment and such evaluation measures as school-wide school climate surveys of students, teachers, and parents; student self-reports; peer reports; and office referrals.
- Develop a clear definition of bullying. Beginning in the earliest grades, embed the prevention of bullying in written policies, including mission statements and the school's code of conduct.
- Increase public awareness of bullying and its negative impact via signs/ posters, assemblies, newsletters, and classroom lessons and discussions on bullying.
- Recognize that bullying is more likely to occur in certain contexts than others (e.g., on playgrounds, buses, and other less supervised settings) and respond accordingly with increased supervision and structured activities in those settings.
- Provide ongoing staff development and training related to all aspects of bullying, including the critical importance of positive teacher-student and student-student relations in preventing bullying.
- Provide skill instruction to students that targets social, emotional, and behavioral aspects of bullying, including those skills for bullies, victims, and bystanders. (e.g., teaching bystanders to "take a stand" against bullying).
- Encourage students not to follow the "code of silence" that supports bullying and reinforce that seeking help is not "snitching." For example, promote slogans such as "friends don't let friends be bullies."
- Provide more intensive interventions to those identified as bullies or who are atrisk of aggression, such as anger management training, mentoring, etc.
- During disciplinary encounters involving bullying, focus not only on the consequences of the behavior for the bully but also on the impact of the behavior on the victim.
- Consider adoption of an evidence-based program that includes the above recommendations, such as *Steps to Respect, BullyProofing Your School,* and *Bullybusters.*

(Consortium To Prevent School Violence, 2010)

Adopting these recommendations can be a step in the right direction toward the prevention of school violence. It is not, however, a solution for all that ails the public school system. We need to continue to be vigilant so that bullying is not present or tolerated within our classrooms. Children as well as adults have to understand that this type of behavior will not be tolerated in a school or workplace.

Being a bully will not be rewarded no matter where you are in America. Bullying will no longer be accepted as a rite of passage or the social norm. It will be seen for what it is: violence toward others, either physically or psychologically. The campaign to end it is underway; it is only a matter of time.

It is well-known that schools need a positive school climate. A positive school climate is characterized by multiple features including an attractive and inviting physical landscape; collaborative relationships among school staff members, students, and families; high expectations for all; an atmosphere of respectful and positive interactions; and opportunities for meaningful participation both academically and socially. In schools with a positive school climate, students tend to be more engaged academically and experience less bullying, crime, general discipline problems, school avoidance, and other social and emotional problems.

Teachers also express greater job satisfaction and commitment to the profession. This is where we must begin in fighting school violence. We must create schools that are welcoming, yet are places of great learning and involvement where both student and faculty want to be part of this environment, as it leads to one achieving and feeling valued. One is able to feel safe and productive.

Research shows that the following characteristics are common among schools that are effective in building and maintaining a positive school climate, as well as in preventing school violence:

Positive relationship-building. Intentional efforts are made to build and maintain caring and supportive relationships among students, teachers, and other school staff members, and families.

Sense of belonging. In addition to positive relationships, both students and staff experience school as meaningful, productive, and relevant. Active student participation in decision making is emphasized, as well as activities such as service learning, which promote a sense of community and belonging.

Positive behavior supports. Emphasis is placed on the use of positive rather than punitive techniques.

High expectations. Teachers, students, and parents expect success in both academic and behavioral endeavors and provide the necessary supports to achieve these expectations.

Social and emotional skills. Deliberate efforts are made to develop social and emotional competencies among all students.

Parent and community involvement. Family and community members are viewed as valuable resources and their active involvement in the school's mission is strongly encouraged.

Fairness and clarity of rules. Students perceive rules as being clear, fair, and not overly harsh.

School safety. Students, teachers, and families perceive the school as safe.

(Consortium to Prevent School Violence, 2010)

If one studies these recommendations, one can quickly ascertain that these are very doable and achievable. They require planning, organization, and leadership. It is a group, as well as an individual, responsibility for success.

School violence is a comprehensive topic that complete books have been written about. I decided to do just a short overview of the topic to begin the awareness that needs to occur when dealing with and understanding some of the future topics discussed in this book. Awareness and comprehension of the magnitude of this topic will enable you the reader to begin to get a sense of this very complicated series of interrelated issues that comprise school violence.

Chapter 3

Psychopathology in Children

Child psychopathology is a manifestation of psychological problems in children. The types of psychological problems can range from oppositional disorder to severe mental illness. The key is to understand that pathology can be present in a variety of children and youth, and it can manifest itself in a variety of ways. This chapter will give an overview of several disorders that constitute a foundation for psychopathology.

REACTIVE ATTACHMENT DISORDER

What is attachment? It is a bond or an emotional connection between the primary caregiver and the infant. The bond affects the child's growth, development, trust, and his or her ability to build relationships. It is a reciprocal relationship and happens after six months of a child's life, but before five years old. There are two types: (a) secure attachment and (b) insecure attachment, an attachment disorder which can be inhibited or uninhibited.

Secure attachment occurs when the primary caregiver consistently responds lovingly to the child's needs such as food, shelter, comfort, sleep, and clothing. The infant experiences the emotional essentials from the primary caregiver such as touch, movement, eye contact, and smiles. This builds trust and is a healthy connection.

Insecure or reactive attachment disorder occurs when there are severely confusing, frightening, and isolating emotional experiences in a child's early years of life that disrupt the bond. The following key factors include multiple caregivers, invasive or painful medical procedures, hospitalization, abuse (sexual, physical, neglect), poor prenatal care (alcohol or drug exposure), neurological

25

problems, a young or inexperienced mother with poor parenting skills, and frequent moves or placements in foster care or institutions. The child learns the world is not a safe place, which results in not trusting and low confidence. The child now has the belief that it is unlovable and will often display similar symptoms of other disorders and may be misdiagnosed with Attention Deficit Disorder, Attention Deficit Hyperactivity Disorder, or Bi-Polar Depression.

The Diagnostic and Statistical Manual of Mental Disorders (DSM-IV) describes "Inhibited Reactive Attachment Disorder as the persistent failure to initiate and respond to most social interactions in a developmentally appropriate way" and "Disinhibited Reactive Attachment Disorder as the display of indiscriminate sociability or a lack of selectivity in the choice of attachment figures (excessive familiarity with relative strangers by making requests and displaying affection)."

A child who experiences Reactive Attachment Disorder may exhibit this list of characteristics:

a) May be aggressive and acts out because of immature fear, hurt, and anger
b) Is excessively clingy and overly demanding
c) Lacks social skills
d) Suffers anxiety or depression
e) Poor eye contact
f) Refusal to answer simple questions
g) Abnormal eating patterns
h) Extreme defiance and control issues
i) Developmentally delayed
j) Destructiveness to self, others, and property
k) Lying about the obvious (crazy lying)
l) Stealing
m) Absence of guilt or remorse
n) Attempts to control attention (usually in a negative way)
o) Poor impulse control
p) Lacks the sense of right and wrong or cause and effect
q) Constant nonsense questions and relentless chatter
   (Children Mental HealthDisorderFactSheet, 2009)

The implications for classroom teachers are numerous in that these early stages of development, which are not adequately developed, create all kinds of challenges for teachers. The lack of adequate or normal experience can result in delays in motor, language, social, and cognitive development.

The child has trouble completing homework, remembering assignments, and has difficulty understanding multiple step assignments. They have problems with comprehension and concentrating. The student has the need to be in control. They show argumentative, defiant behavior, which disrupts the classroom and turns into a power struggle with teachers.

There are some suggested instructional practices that are recommended for this type of student experiencing this level of pathology. To respond with an effective intervention, you need to understand the purpose or function of the behavior. A Functional Behavioral Assessment (FBA) should be considered. Model and teach social skills.

Natural Consequences are important. Time-outs do not work. Try "time-ins," which have the child sit alongside of you while you explain how much fun the other children are having. Avoid power struggles with the student. Use humor when appropriate. Do not phrase demands in a question. Allow a response time before repeating the demand. Give choices. Always remain calm and in control of yourself. Make sure to acknowledge good decisions and good behaviors. Instill in the student the understanding that their behavior is their choice.

Classroom accommodations are also needed to help this child be successful. Break down assignments that are difficult. Also help with clarification and multiple-step directions. Being consistent, repetitive, and predictable gives the student the feeling of security and safety, which reduces anxiety and fear.

Create an environment that is highly structured. Set boundaries in the classroom. Be sensitive to changes in schedule, transitions, surprises, and chaotic social situations. Identify a break area or a place the student can go to during times of frustration and anxiety. Make sure it is a supervised location. Set limits to breaks, such as three minutes or ten deep breaths (Center for Family Development, 2010).

ANTISOCIAL PERSONALITY
(OPPOSITIONAL DEFIANCE) DISORDER

Individuals with Antisocial Behavior Disorder or Oppositional Defiance Disorder regularly disregard and violate the rights of others, exhibit aggressive or destructive behaviors, break laws or rules, and act deceitful or steal. There are two types of antisocial behavior: *Overt* involves acts against people. *Covert* involves acts against property or self-abuse.

Children with Antisocial Behavior Disorder can be identified very accurately at age 3 or 4. There are some very specific symptoms associated with Antisocial Personality Disorder: Failure to conform to social norms, deceitfulness, impulsivity, irritability and aggressiveness, reckless disregard, consistent irresponsibility, and lack of remorse.

There is a developmental progression of antisocial personality disorder. At the ages of three to six, we see a series of oppositional symptoms manifest themselves: stubbornness, defiance of adults, noncompliance, temper tantrums, irritability, arguments with adults, blame for others, being annoying to others, spitefulness, and anger.

At the ages of seven to nine years, we see the onset of early conduct disorder symptoms manifesting themselves in the increased severity of the types of behaviors that are now present. We start to observe lying, physical fighting, bullying others, setting fires, swearing, cruelty to animals, and breaking rules.

Once puberty and/or adolescence begins, at ages ten to fourteen, we start to see severe conduct disorder types of behavior: cruelty to others, stealing, running away from home, truancy, breaking and entering, and sometimes raping of younger children. Most children diagnosed with Antisocial Behavior Disorder are boys.

Antisocial Behavior Disorder in girls is more often self-directed than outer-directed. Antisocial behavior early in a child's school career is the best indicator of delinquency in adolescence. At least 70 percent of antisocial youth have been arrested at least once within three years of leaving school. Children and youth who are at risk for antisocial behavior patterns are also at risk for: academic failure, child abuse and neglect, drug and alcohol involvement, sexually transmitted diseases, accidents, tobacco use, gang membership and delinquency.

It is unfortunate, but the prognosis for these children is not very promising once they have entered the arena of antisocial personality behavior disorders. "Kids with Oppositional Defiance Disorder are essentially handicapped in their ability to be flexible and handle frustration."

> "These kids maintain an oppositional attitude even when it's clearly not in their best interest, so we have to assume they would be doing well if they could, but they lack the capacity for flexibility and frustration management that ordinary children develop."
>
> *Ross W. Greene*

Strategies that have been known to be effective in schools with this population are be proactive, redirect, don't take the behavior personally, refuse to join the fight, use simple enforceable consequences, give child or youth choices for preferred outcome, and involve and educate parents about consistent practices that can be done at school and at home. Overall, praise the small accomplishments—it begins there.

CONDUCT DISORDERS

Conduct Disorder is generally used to describe a pattern of repeated and persistent misbehavior. This misbehavior is much worse than would normally be expected in a child of that age. Children and adolescents with this disorder have great difficulty following rules and behaving in a socially acceptable way. They are often viewed by other children, adults, and social agencies as "bad" or delinquent, rather than mentally ill. Terms used to describe conduct disordered children and youth are; disobedient, antisocial, aggressive, oppositional, defiant, delinquent, and challenging.

The common behaviors are:

Aggressive conduct: Aggression toward people and animals.
Nonaggressive conduct: Destruction of property.
Deceitfulness or theft conduct: Deceitfulness, lying, or stealing.
Serious violations of rules conduct: Violation of parental, societal, or school rules.
Conduct disorders rarely exist by themselves. There is often co-morbidity with the following conditions: Attention Deficit Disorder, Learning, Anxiety, Mood, and Communication Disorders. At times, depressive symptoms and alcohol and drug abuse will lead to more acting out behaviors.

Onset of conduct disorders may occur as early as age 5 or 6, but more usually occurs in late childhood or early adolescence; onset after the age of 16 is rare. It has been shown that when treated, most children and adolescents do not grow up to have behavioral problems or problems with the law. Most youth do well as adults, both socially and occupationally. There are both genetic and environmental components to conduct disorders, which are more common among children of adults with exhibited conduct problems.

Some of the possible causes of conduct disorders are: Neurological Dysregulation, Child Biological Factors, School-Related Factors, Parent Psychological Factors, divorce, marital distress, marital violence, life stressors, parent and child interactions, and family characteristics. There are five aspects of parenting that are more commonly associated with conduct disorders. They are poor supervision, erratic harsh discipline, parental disharmony, rejections of the child, and low parental involvement in child's activities.

Conduct is usually diagnosed if the following are present:

There is a repetitive and persistent pattern of behavior where age-appropriate norms or rules are violated.

Three or more characteristic behaviors have been present during the past twelve months, or one behavior in the last six months.

Disturbance must cause clinically significant impairment in social, academic, or occupational functioning.

Conduct disordered youth often will manifest neurological patterns of aggression. Over-aroused aggression is aggression resulting from heightened arousal and activity levels, not characterized by intent to inflict pain or by attempts to use aggression for instrumental purposes. Impulsive aggression is aggression that occurs in a sudden burst, without any identifiable precursors or signs.

Affective aggression is also aggression that occurs in a sudden burst, without any identifiable precursors or signs. However, it is aggression arising out of states of intense anger and rage, and includes violent episodes and highly destructive behavior. Predatory aggression is aggression associated with a thought disorder involving paranoia where individuals misinterpret neutral social behavior directed toward them as intentionally harmful. Instrumental aggression is aggression that uses aggressive tactics to maximize an individual's advantage to get their way through intimidation, humiliation, and coercion.

Differences between conduct disordered girls and boys are easily identifiable. Boys are more likely to express their antisocial behavior in confrontational, externalizing forms; girls are more covert and internalizing. Antisocial girls have more psychological symptoms and tend to have higher rates of DSM-IV disorders than boys. Antisocial girls also have higher rates of physical, emotional, and sexual abuse. They suffer more neglect, and have increased incidence of family histories of mental illness.

The timing of when the problem behaviors begin will have lasting impact. Early starters are socialized to antisocial behavior from infancy by the family environment and family stressors that disrupt parenting practices. Early starters are substantially more at risk for a host of adjustment problems than late starters. Late starters are socialized to antisocial behavior by peer group influences.

Schools that are more successful with conduct disordered students are more likely to have structured curriculum and clearly defined expectations. The faculty usually receives professional development and incidents are processed effectively and with a high degree of fidelity of implementation. The programs are challenging yet integrated in the life of the students.

In the last ten years, schools have become more aware of how to deal effectively with this type of pathology. Schools have used Primary prevention, which is an intervention effort designed to keep problems from emerging. Secondary prevention intervention efforts seek to reverse harm to children and youth who already exhibit the behavioral signs of prior risk exposure. Tertiary prevention-intervention efforts seek to reduce harm for the most severely involved at-risk children and youth.

Parental involvement is a key to effective collaboration between home and school. Parent involvement in the planning and implementation of school interventions is crucial. Many of the adjustment problems that antisocial students experience at school have their origins in the home. The more settings there are in which interventions for antisocial behavior can be implemented, the more likely there is to be a substantive, overall impact on students' total behavior.

Parental support in coordinating the school and home components of an intervention can significantly increase the effectiveness of any school intervention.

Parent involvement sometimes opens the door for parent education that can lead to more effective parenting practices, more positive parent-child interactions, and improved student self-esteem. The school can help the parent provide encouragement and discipline at home. Specific skills can be taught to the parent on how to cope with noncompliance, and further education and support can prevent abuse.

There are a variety of effective interventions for conduct disordered children and youth. Most common are Behavioral Therapy, Cognitive Behavioral approaches, medication, psychotherapy, and functional family therapy.

OBSESSIVE-COMPULSIVE PERSONALITY DISORDER

OCD is characterized by recurrent obsessions and/or compulsions that are intense enough to cause severe discomfort. Obsessions are recurrent and persistent thoughts, impulses, or images that are unwanted cause marked anxiety or stress. Compulsions are repetitive behaviors or rituals (like hand washing, checking something over and over) or mental acts (counting, repeating words silently, avoiding). OCD is a brain disorder and tends to run in the family.

In childhood OCD, a family history of the disorder is more frequent than in adult onset OCD, with genetic factors playing more of a role in childhood OCD. Recent studies have shown that OCD may develop or worsen after a strep infection. Most children go through developmental stages characterized by compulsive behaviors and rituals that are normal. For example: boys thinking girls have "cooties" or collecting things.

Superstitions are forms of "magical thinking" in which children believe in the power of their thoughts or actions to control events in the world. Examples of this would be lucky numbers or rhymes such as "Step on a crack, break your momma's back." Normal rituals advance development, enhance socialization, and help children deal with separation anxiety and will disappear with age.

Rituals of the child with OCD persist well into adulthood. They are painful, disabling, and result in feelings of shame and isolation. Attempts to stop doing the rituals result in extreme anxiety. Some of the characteristics that seem to be very common are being overly concerned with dirt or germs (frequent hand washing), long and frequent trips to the bathroom, avoiding playgrounds and messy art projects, especially stickiness.

OCD children have an insistence on having things in a certain order. They have "safe" or "bad numbers" and will often have repeating rituals, for example, going in and out of doors a certain way, taking excessive time to perform tasks, excessive hoarding or collecting, unexplained absences from school, rereading and rewriting, and repetitively erasing their work till it often is damaged beyond repair.

Children don't always recognize that they have a problem. Intervention in the form of a combination of medication and cognitive-behavior therapy is often the most effective treatment. Family support and education are also central to the success of the treatments. Medication should only be considered when children are experiencing significant OCD-related impairment or distress. Seven medications make up the first line of defense for OCD. They are Anafranil, Prozac, Zoloft, Paxil, Luvox, Lexapro, and Celexa. It can take up to twelve weeks to determine if medication is going to work.

Cognitive behavioral therapy is another intervention that has proven success. It is an action-oriented approach to help children confront their fears and learn more appropriate responses to fear-provoking situations. At the same time, a therapist works with the child to limit or even stop the compulsive behaviors that they are exhibiting. Eventually, the child will learn to tolerate their disorder without having to resort to compulsive behaviors.

Children are in schools every day, so it is important that the educators that work with these OCD children have strategies/interventions. Teachers can be attentive to changes in a student's behavior. They can allow the student to turn in late work for full credit. Educate student's peers about OCD. Post a daily schedule in a highly visible place. Try to redirect student behavior. Try to accommodate situations and behaviors that the student has no control over. Have the student work with a partner so they stay on task. Identify the student's strengths and talents. Be aware of any peer problems or emotional needs of the student. Allow more time for completing tasks and tests.

Children with OCD can be successful in school and in life provided that they are given the right types of supports and intervention. One of the major interventions is adult education about the disorder. In that way the adult can be informed about what to do, what to expect, and what to overlook. Awareness of this disorder can create an atmosphere where the student is successful or the obsessive behaviors control the environment and the child and teacher are both unsuccessful at navigating the daily waters of public school education.

SCHIZOPHRENIA

Schizophrenia is a serious brain disorder. It is a disease that makes it difficult for a person to tell the difference between real and unreal experiences, to think logically, to have normal emotional responses to others, and to behave normally in social situations. Suicide is a serious danger in people with schizophrenia. About 10 percent of people with schizophrenia commit suicide. Young adult males are at highest risk. If a person with schizophrenia mentions suicide or seems suicidal, contact the doctor immediately.

Contrary to popular belief, it does not involve a "Jekyll-and-Hyde" type of split personality. Schizophrenia literally means "a split mind," and this may be where the misconception of split personality took root. In the United States, about 3 million people have this illness. About 80 percent of people with schizophrenia can live either full, productive lives or relatively independent lives with treatment. Early treatment of schizophrenia and newer treatment options may control the illness in up to 85 percent of individuals.

The causes of schizophrenia are well documented. There are 4 areas that have received the most amount of research attention and multiple studies have come to the same conclusions.

Heredity—Schizophrenia runs in some families. A person can inherit a tendency to develop the illness, especially if a parent has the disorder. The risk for inheriting schizophrenia is 10 percent in those who have an immediate family member with the illness, and 40 percent if the illness affects either parent or an identical twin. However, about 60 percent of people with schizophrenia have no close relatives with the illness.

Brain chemistry—Many researchers believe that people with schizophrenia are either very sensitive to a brain chemical called dopamine or produce too much of it. Dopamine is a neurotransmitter, which is a substance that allows nerve cells in the brain to send messages to each other. An imbalance of this chemical can affect the way a person's brain reacts to stimuli.

Brain abnormality—Better imaging technology has allowed researchers to study the brain structure and function in people with schizophrenia. They have concluded that many individuals with the disorder have subtle abnormalities in brain structure. These abnormalities include a slight enlargement of the fluid-filled cavities (ventricles) in the brain, and a slightly smaller size of some areas of the brain. But this is not true in all people with schizophrenia, and such abnormalities also have been identified in people who do not have schizophrenia.

Complications during pregnancy and birth—Some researchers believe that an infection or malnutrition during pregnancy, or complications during birth, may increase the chances of that child developing schizophrenia when he or she is older.

Schizophrenia affects about one percent of all people. Schizophrenia affects individuals who span the full range of intelligence and education. A person is at higher risk for developing schizophrenia if they are a male between the ages of 15 and 24, are a female between the ages of 25 and 34, have a close relative with the illness, or had a medical problem surrounding their birth. Schizophrenia runs in some families.

The symptoms of schizophrenia vary from one person to another, and those symptoms can appear either gradually or suddenly. At first, symptoms may include mild feelings of tension, inability to sleep or concentrate, and a loss of interest in school, work, or friends. Early warning signs of schizophrenia in children include trouble distinguishing dreams from reality, confusing television or movies with reality, seeing things and hearing voices that are not real, confused thinking, extreme moodiness, a belief that people are "out to get them," behaving younger than one's age, severe anxiety and fearfulness, or severe problems in making and keeping friends.

Educational intervention for children with schizophrenia is nearly impossible to describe because the symptoms and educational needs of these students vary so greatly. However, classroom teachers are not helpless—they can use some of the following strategies within the classroom. Recognize the early warning signs, bring the illness into the open, reduce stress, help set realistic goals, work together "child's team," make modifications to insure success, notify school personnel, know the facts, and make the student feel accepted.

When special education is necessary, it appears that a highly structured, individualized program provides a feeling of safety and allows the student to keep symptoms in check as much as possible. Children with schizophrenia need comprehensive treatment plans involving other professionals. A combination of medication and individual therapy, feeling therapy, and specialized programs (school, activities, etc.) is often necessary.

SELF-INJURY/SELF MUTILATION

In the last fifteen years a whole new disorder has come to light. Youth are manifesting this pathology in self-injury. This is the intentional, direct injuring of body tissue without suicidal intent. It is an impulsive act to regulate mood. The most common form of self-harm is cutting, but self-harm also covers a wide range of behaviors, including burning, sniffing, bruising, scratching, banging or hitting body parts, interfering with wound healing, self-embedding of objects, hair pulling and the ingestion of toxic substances or objects.

Cutting is often a secretive activity. It is usually done to an area that is easily reached such as the arms, legs, or torsos. It is often concealed by clothing. It is explained away by rational excuses when noticed by others.

The group who is most at risk is primarily adolescent females as well as some males. Youth with a history of sexual abuse or trauma as a child, coexisting psychiatric disorders (addiction, borderline personality disorder, conduct disorder, depression, eating disorders); those who lack social support and who lack coping skills have low self-esteem or a desire to be perfect and have impulse control issues are excellent candidates.

What are the warning signs? Adults who work with adolescents can be vigilant for the following warning signs: unexplained cuts; associating with peers who cut themselves; signs of depression or poor self-esteem; frequent accidents; changes in eating habits; covering arms, legs and wrists—even in hot weather; and being in frequent possession of weapons or sharp tools.

How prevalent is self-injury? Cutting is the most prevalent form of non-suicidal self-injury. It appears to be increasing in prevalence. In the United States, estimates are 1 in 200 girls between the ages of 13 and 19 years old cut themselves! In the past, it was thought that teen girls were more likely to self-injure than boys. Recent studies indicate that the numbers are equal (www.teenhelp.com).

Why do students self-injure? They may lack healthy outlets such as group sports and creative hobbies, which help to diffuse tension and stress. Self-injury becomes a maladaptive coping strategy to help a teen release tension and stress through physical relief. Injuring one's self actually releases endorphins, causing temporary relief from emotional pain. One must cut over and over again to get continued relief. It may be a distraction from pain or anger, a way to feel something "real." It is not always the case that they self-injure for extra attention. Many feel shameful about the act and work to conceal the evidence.

Hicks and Hinck (2009) have formulated best practice intervention for care of clients who self- mutilate. Their intervention has three steps:

1. The provider's self-evaluation of values beliefs and assumptions
2. Client assessment
3. Therapeutic strategies (emotional, social, and biological)

Emotional strategies: counseling, journaling and creative activities to learn how to express feelings safely and productively.

Social strategies: activities to change behavior such as contracts, cognitive therapy, assertiveness training and problem solving.

Biological strategies: finding natural ways to release endorphins such as exercise.

Pharmacological agents may also be used.

What can educators do? Intervene early. Self-mutilators are more receptive to help during the early stages of the disorder. Help students to desensitize to social situations if the cutting is due to social anxiety. Be friendly, patient, positive, and empathetic. Recognize your own prejudices and preconceptions about self-injury.

Be careful not to reinforce cutting by providing extra attention for cutting; instead, try to reinforce positive coping behaviors. Provide opportunities for students to choose assignments that are less likely to produce anxiety. Limit surprises in class by giving students warnings before tests and assignments. Assist with time management for longer assignments and provide support as needed. Recognize that students may experience side effects such as fatigue, weight gain, and inattention on psychiatric medications.

The important things to remember with this group is that self-injury is preventable and with the right type of cognitive restructuring and problem solving skills this individual can successfully resolve many of the problems facing them as a teen in today's world. It is not hopeless, which is how they often will feel. There are solutions.

EXPLOSIVE PERSONALITY DISORDER

Explosive Personality Disorder is an impulse control disorder character- ized by episodes of aggressive, destructive behavior resulting in damage to an individual or property. It is also called Intermittent Explosive Disorder (IED). The outburst can occur with little or no provocation. The aggressive, destructive feelings and behavior appear very suddenly and subside almost as quickly. They are often followed by regret or embarrassment over lack of self-control and the resulting damage. The aggressive episodes typically last about twenty minutes and generally occur from one to twenty-five times a month.

Impulsive aggression is a primitive response driven by fear or anger (or a distortion of environmental circumstances) as seen in animal populations. IED and other impulse control issues may be linked in large part to bipolar disorder and serotonin levels in the brain. Explosive Personality Disorder, or IED, tends to be more frequently observed in males than females. Inter- mittent Explosive Symptoms have been observed in premenstrual women. Between 11 percent and 18 percent of people qualify for the IED diagnosis at some point in their life. Highest prevalence found to be in younger, less- educated, African-American and Hispanic, males. Symptoms are observed to appear an average of 6 years earlier in males than females (age 13 as opposed to 19).

DSM-IV Criteria for Intermittent Explosive Disorder

A. Several discrete episodes of failure to resist aggressive impulses that result in serious assaultive acts or destruction of property.

B. The degree of aggressiveness expressed during the episodes is grossly out of proportion to any psychosocial stressor.

C. The aggressive behaviors are not better accounted for by another mental disorder and are not the direct physiological effect of a substance or general medical condition (From the Diagnostic and Statistical Manual of Mental Disorders, Fourth Edition, Text Revision. 2000 American Psychiatric Association).

The effects on the educator and at school or in the classroom are major. The course of this illness is episodic and unpredictable. It requires the teacher or aides to establish a rapport with the student. The educator must pick up on antecedents and must have developed a safety plan with the student. Educators must provide a safe environment to handle an episode. Students in class bear witness to these episodes and could suffer lasting traumatic effects.

There is a physical attack with a primary victim, where the student is at the receiving end of the explosive child. There are emotional primary and secondary victims (bystanders) who bear witness to the assaults and are impacted in numerous ways.

There are possible pre-escalation interventions—for instance, during stable functioning. The adult can reduce the amount of stimuli on the student. They can regulate the environment to reduce stress, frustration, anger, and so on. There can be a reduced emphasis on competition. Teacher and peers can model socially acceptable behavior to explosive students.

Educators can provide the student with opportunities for both social and academic success. It is imperative that the teacher have a detailed list of expectations for both the student and other teachers that enter the room or teach that particular group of students. Teachers can also provide ample processing time before transitions, and settle time after a transition. Above all else, the main thing is consistency, consistency, and more consistency.

There are Crisis and Post-Crisis Interventions that have proven to be successful as well. Remove the student from the group until they can display appropriate/safe behavior. Treat the student with dignity. Be consistent with consequences. Maintain a "flat affect" when intervening. Intervene early when there is a problem.

Medications and drug treatment specific to IED has not been studied in great depth yet, but a number of medications used to reduce aggression are available. Antidepressants (e.g., Prozac), mood stabilizers (e.g., Lithium), and antipsychotic drugs are just several examples. Medications bring out many ethical concerns and may have severe and sometimes lasting sideeffects and should be used with caution.

MEAN GIRL SYNDROME

"Relational Aggression(or 'Covert bullying') is associated with the formation of social cliques and the subtle and cruel verbal and psychological tactics girls may use to injure another child's feelings of social acceptance"(O'Neil, 2008). It includes social isolation or exclusion, exploitation of a friendship or alliance building, manipulative affection, teasing, taunting or insulting, gossiping and spreading rumors, ignoring, staring or giving nasty looks, stealing friends or boyfriends, and cyber-bullying.

Why do young adolescent females exhibit these types of behavior? The reasons are as individual as the individual girl—it can be out of fear, a need for power and control, social dominance, security, or popularity. Girls learn very young, through adult feedback, to develop interpersonal and social skills, ensure that their interactions have peaceful outcomes, and practice cooperation and communication in play.

Young girls are typically most comfortable playing in pairs or small groups. They quickly learn to "read" their playmates' nonverbal communication, such as intonation, flip of the hair, cock of the head, or body positioning. This sets the foundation for female interactions later in life.

Nonverbal communication can convey an array of messages, and to another girl can be just as clear as the spoken or written word. They can convey messages such as superiority, power, disdain or disagreement, and covert aggression.

The nature of girls' early friendships may also serve as training for later heterosexual dating relationships: "There is usually an open show of affection between these little girls—both physically in the form of handholding and verbally through 'love notes' that reaffirm how special each is to the other" (Lever, 1976: 484 as cited by O'Neil).

Girls' intimate relationships with their friends often cultivate similar jealous and possessive feelings commonly associated with immature romantic relationships. Girls' friendships are often dissolved for reasons similar to romantic "breakups." It often centers around the introduction of a third girl to the relationship that one girl feels threatened by, or a perceived act of disloyalty. Girls often carry this "breakup" mentality to their adolescent or teen relationships, further setting the stage for relational aggression.

The nature of adolescent girls' friendships is quite complex and transitional. Parents are no longer the primary source of social support. The girl begins to rely on peers for social support and values being accepted within a social group. Her peers attribute strongly to self-concept. Female adolescent relationships are generally unstable. Around the age of nine, the young girl begins to realize the power she has over the emotions and relationships of others.

Most report the breaking of a friendship as the most anxiety-provoking aspect of school life. A commonly reported reason for the breaking of friendships was the presence of another girl entering, or attempting to enter, into a female relationship being perceived as a threat or breaking trust, such as sharing another's secret.

There exists a hierarchy of power within these adolescent female relationships. Each individual is assigned a role within this existing system or group. The roles are common in that there is the queen, the sidekick, the gossiper, the floater, the torn bystander, "the wannabe," and the target.

The Queen

- Friends do what she wants
- Charming to adults
- Manipulatively affectionate
- Doesn't take responsibility
- Judges peers by loyalty and threat

The Sidekick

- Feels the Queen is the authority.
- Gets pushed around by the Queen
- Will lie for Queen

The Floater

- Moves freely among groups
- Doesn't want to exclude people
- Avoids conflicts
- Higher self-esteem
- Not competitive

The Gossip

- Extremely secretive
- Friends with everyone
- Good Communicator
- Seemingly nice and trustworthy
- Uses others' secrets to advantage
- Rarely excluded from the group

Torn Bystander

- Often forced to choose between friends
- Accommodating
- Peacemaker
- Doormat

The Target

- May have fallen from higher rank
- Feels helpless and alone
- Masks hurt feelings
- Feels vulnerable and humiliated
- May try to change to fit in

The "Wannabe"

- Others' opinions and wants dictate
- Desperate to fit in
- Likes "helping" other girls
- Loves to gossip
- Future implications
- Every Girl Needs . . .
- Social Inclusion
- Positive Sense of Self
- Developing Friendships
- Positive Communication
- Personal Interactions
  (Relational Aggression: More than Just Mean Girls)

It is interesting to note that the girls seem to understand their assigned or chosen roles clearly and are often vested in keeping their positions in fear of suddenly falling from grace and becoming the next victim. Research has shown that depending on the role the young female is playing, there are serious adjustment consequences that seem to follow.

The bully has some serious adjustment problems, such as anxiety and depression, poor relational skills, later delinquent and criminal behavior, early dating, sexuality, victimization, and unplanned pregnancies later in life.

The victim also experiences serious adjustment problems such as anxiety and depression, feelings of loneliness and isolation, poor relational skills, inability to trust, suicide, later delinquent and criminal behavior, sexual victimization and unplanned pregnancies, poor grades, diminished educational experience, distorted sense of self, diminished sense of worth, self-injury, and substance abuse or addictions.

The bystanders also experience anxiety, have a diminished educational experience and feelings of guilt or shame for not intervening to rescue or help the victim. All three players in this situation end up losing. They are all victims in one way or another. The ability to be untouched by the mean girl syndrome is very unlikely as it alive and well in today's schools.

Why is this type of pathology so hard to detect? Relational Aggression is very hard for an untrained observer to spot. It generally appears to be normal squabbles among girls. Victims are reluctant to share an incident for many reasons, such as fear of retaliation and further isolation; if it is a friendship "breaking up," she might have feelings of loyalty and hope for it to be repaired.

Psychological or emotional abuse is harder to prove and can cause mental doubt and self-blame. Bullies generally focus on an aspect of the victim's appearance or personality. The victim may agree with the bully's criticism, leaving her powerless to complain. Bystanders are generally reluctant to report Relational Aggression, or to intervene on the victim's behalf out of fear of becoming the next target.

Cyber-bullying: Cyber-bullying fits the nature of girls and "Relational Aggression," making it an ever-growing tool of choice for girls. The reasons are numerous in that there is anonymity behind screen name, ability to distance themselves and feeling less empathy. Lack of rules and regulations indicates a lesser chance of being found out and fits the covert nature of relational aggression. Social networking and chat rooms plays directly to the "Means Girls" interest in socially undermining the victim. It is extremely efficient. The bully can spread gossip, rumors, and insults to a greater number of people very quickly.

What can schools do? Include "Relational Aggression" to the School's "anti-bullying policy." Set clear consequences and provide a safe system of reporting acts of bullying. Develop a school-wide understanding of "Relational Aggression" and a common language to describe the behaviors. Create a school culture that understands the unstable nature of female relationships, and can identify the difference between developmental friction and unnecessary hurtful acts. Include diversity and empathy training. Create an environment and system where victims can safely receive help.

Schools can use and relate to the numerous resources now available to set policy, and teach awareness, coping skills, and strategies. Practice and teach computer safety. Extend education to parents. Listen, communicate, and observe student interactions. Provide extracurricular activities that will allow girls to build self-esteem, while getting to know girls outside of her social circle.

This phenomenon will continue to plague our schools unless educators, parents, and community agencies rally to make it unacceptable and provide natural consequences for this type of behavior. There have been instances of mean girl syndrome as early as 3–4 years in preschool and in kindergarten classes. We need to get this under control and provide these young females with problem and communication skills so they are better able to navigate their human and personal relationships.

ABUSE

Child abuse and psychopathology seem to go hand in hand. Abuse is defined in the following ways:

Physical Abuse—A nonaccidental injury.

Child Neglect—Failure to meet the basic needs of a child.

Sexual Abuse—Sexual involvement imposed on a child by an adult or older child.

Emotional Abuse—Not providing an emotional atmosphere in which children can develop normally.

Combination child abuse is typically more common than single child abuse. A physically abused child may also be an emotionally abused child. Children at any age may experience child abuse.

Indicators: Physical Abuse

Physical: Bruises—different colors and/or shapes. Burns—cigarette shape, immersions.
Behavioral: Socially withdrawn. Arrives to school early—leaves late.
Emotional: Fears adults. Depression.

Indicators: Sexual Abuse

Physical: Stomach and headaches. Genital pains/itching/odors.
Behavioral: Preoccupied/Knowledge of sex. Poor peer relations.
Emotional: Depression/guilt. Hostility/Anger—Tantrums.

Indicators: Child Neglect

Physical: Poor Hygiene—drowsy. Malnutrition—obesity, frequently hungry.
Behavioral: Begs for food. Impaired socialization.
Emotional: Anxiety. Hostility.

Indicators: Emotional Abuse

Physical: Delayed development. Poor physical appearance.
Behavioral: Poor peer relationships. Self-destructive acts.
Emotional: Anxiety. Emotional extremes.

Environmental factors may also play a role in whether abuse occurs. The following factors have been proven to encourage abuse: Social isolation, and domestic abuse such as family stresses—unemployment, financial problems, lack of childcare and a past history of abuse, with unrealistic expectation of the child that lead to the child never quite measuring up or meeting expectations. Parents who experience difficulty in caring for special needs children that have a multiple needs and there is no support available, and or very small children where the adult is not able to regulate or soothe the upset child or understand what is truly happening within the child.

Although research links sexual abuse to psychopathology, the complexity of children's lives is such that this is but one factor that may lead to acting out behaviors. Sexually abused children are the ones that are the most frequently referred to psychological mental services because of the possible acting out that may occur because of the abuse.

Often sexually abused children are also exposed to family problems, substance abuse, prior maltreatment, and domestic violence which also pose threats to their mental health and their potential for lashing out aggressively or violently. Research has also shown that children's sexual abuse experiences vary greatly and that not all children will experience the same level of psychological or pathological problems. It has been documented that if there are strong emotional supports available to children following the abuse such as from a nonoffending caregiver or other adult, the child is less likely to exhibit disturbing behavioral patterns.

Sexual abuse accompanied by neglect is associated with higher levels of internalizing behavior problems. Sexual abuse along with physical and emotional abuse, family disruption, and poverty predicted the most clinical depression and anxiety in the victims. Depressed adolescents who experience both types of abuse exhibit the most symptoms of pathology and interpersonal violence. Research has indicated that the worst psychological outcomes are to be expected among children who experience a longer duration of abuse, abuse by a parental perpetrator, and abuse that involves more invasive sexual acts.

Abuse is a crime against children and robs them of their childhood. It often prevents the individual from forming lasting and healthy relationships with adults. The abuse seems to rear its ugliness in a variety of ways. Abuse is a lifelong experience that is a memory that is forever present. We cannot

predict with a level of certainty whether the victim will be able to comprehend and move forward or that the individual will be forever damaged and
will lash out in multiple ways toward a variety of individuals that are part of
his or her inner circle. There are many stories of victory over abuse and there
is hope that one day abuse will not be part of the childhood experience for
anyone.

Chapter 4

Juvenile Fire Starters

A fire starter is defined as any child that frequently plays with matches or lighters or who has started fires in or outside of the home. Fire starters are not limited to any race, gender, or economic status.

"Juveniles account for more than 50% of all arson arrests in the U.S." (Burn Institute).

"Children playing with fire cause nearly 80,000 structure fires per year which result in approximately 760 deaths and more than 3,500 injuries" (Burn Institute).

There is an estimated $2 billion in damages caused each year by child fire-play" (Melissa Dittman).

"It takes 2 minutes for a match to set an entire room on fire and 5 minutes for a whole house" (Burn Institute).

Arson is the number one crime committed by juveniles. One-third of all children killed by fire set the fire themselves, and 81 percent of all fire starters will repeat, if not treated. These staggering statistics make public and school officials pay attention.

A four-year-old boy set a stuffed animal ablaze as he played with a lighter on his bed. He then shut his bedroom door behind him and joined his family for dinner, leaving the room to burn. Within twenty minutes, the smoke detector blared. The house filled with smoke, and the boy's bedroom was engulfed in flames, causing $100,000 in damages. Later, when a psychologist asked the boy why he didn't tell anyone about the fire, he replied, "I thought if I closed the door it would go away" (Melissa Dittmann).

There are many incidents where children have set fires. Here are several situations as recounted by Melissa Dittman and her research: "In Rochester, New York, a two-year-old, playing with matches started a fire that took his life and the lives of five family members." "In Roanoke, Virginia, a seven-year-old boy set fire to a chair in an abandoned building; the fire spread to an adjacent house and trapped an elderly woman."

"In Passaic, New Jersey, a firefighter was killed and hundreds of people lost their homes in a fire started by a group of teenage boys. These tragic events are not isolated" (Melissa Dittman). All of these situations just confirm the fact that children need to be monitored and supervised consistently and frequently.

There are different types of fire starters. They are the Curious, Crisis, and Delinquent fire starters. Curious Fire Starters are young children between the ages of three and seven. They set impulsive fires using matches or lighters left in easy reach. This group is often left unsupervised and fire starting materials are easily within reach. There is often little intent but more fascination and curiosity with the flames, not with the power of the flame.

The curiosity with fire is the function of the behavior. They truly have a lack of understanding fire's danger. Also due to their young age they are unable to process the full capacity of what fire can do and the damage it may cause. The exploration with the matches can lead to severe burns which ends the playing with fire. The fire setter in this stage often outgrows the fascination and is often treated with fire safety education. Seventy percent of all fire-starters fall into the curious fire setter category.

Crisis Fire Starters use fires to bring attention to problems that they are dealing with. Such problems include changes in the family, school problems, or a crisis or some kind of trauma or recent change in family life, parental alcoholism or drug abuse, or attachment problems. This individual is often reacting to these environmental stressors. They set the fires as a way of getting attention, seeking revenge or having adults take notice of this emotional trauma or hardship.

Pathological Fire Starters

These delinquent fire starters are often adolescents between the ages of twelve and eighteen. They have a history of behavioral problems and usually have poor peer relationships, experience social isolation, and are being bullied by their peers. In addition, they often have a history of physical, emotional, or sexual abuse or neglect. Bedwetting continues way beyond what is developmentally appropriate, with some continuing to wet the bed up to age sixteen.

Experts at blaming others or unwilling to accept responsibility for their own actions, they generally lack empathy and therefore are able to continue to destroy property without any guilt whatsoever. If they happen to find like-minded peers they will set vandalism fires, sometimes in groups. They will seek out trash containers, old warehouses, and garages, and will set them on fire just for the thrill of it. Lacking in responsible decision making, they cannot recognize the results or consequences of their actions and do not worry about the consequences or impact of their actions on others. This group requires a psychologist to screen for depression, conduct, or aggression issues.

Treatments would require cognitive and behavioral therapy, at times while incarcerated, as many of them will not see that they have any type of difficulty or dysfunction in their behavior. Family therapy is encouraged but often unsuccessful if the parent does not have full control and fails to monitor the youth frequently and consistently.

Environmental Fire Starters

This group of fire starters has a different pathology than the pathological fire starters. This group seems to set fires as a response to events happening in that youth's life. Often the fire starting is due to the following factors: lack of parental supervision, peer influence, or exposure to fire early in life. Due to the fact that these environmental factors can be regulated, the youth is more likely to terminate his activities.

Intervention would require child, parental, and peer educational programs. Fire education through local fire departments can be easily accessed, and fire safety day in schools can lead to better awareness and understanding about how fire needs to be respected and that fire safety is an absolute necessity in one's life.

MOTIVATION FOR FIRE STARTING

Why start fires? Youths start fires for reasons as numerous as the youths themselves. The function of the behavior can have multiple areas. Social issues (lack of peer relationships, low self-esteem) are often primary areas where a youth will experience issues. This feeling of being isolated or an outcast will encourage the acting out behavior.

The lack of connection and belongingness will make it easier to set the fire, and the destruction is easier to rationalize when the victims are not your friends. "They don't like you anyway, so it does not matter if you destroy everything they value or own" is the predominant thought running through the fire starter's mind.

There is often a history of abuse (physical, emotional, or sexual), with the fire starter possibly having been the victim of abuse. The only solution to ending the abuse is to destroy the environment where the abuse may be happening. The youth believes that by starting fire to the house, the abuser will no longer have a place to abuse them. They will be freed and cleansed by the fire.

This abused youth has been victimized for years before starting fire to the house. Youths who have suffered abuse need all of the available supports and resources to protect them and give them the psychological and mental health services that they require to return to normal functioning.

A history of behavioral issues (including deviant behavior) completes the profile. The youths have a history of small petty crimes, run-ins with the law, and interactions with the juvenile justice system. Many of these youths have been involved in conflicts with authority figures and as a form of retaliation have set fires. The fires set by this group are usually revenge motivated.

It is a form of justice and equalizing the playing field, as well as serving as a warning to the adults or authority figures. Their past history of oppositional behaviors is well-documented. Unfortunately, this group often has poor coping skills and even poorer problem-solving skills. Their repertoire consists of defiance and acting out, followed by fire starting.

Lack of fire safety knowledge is very common. When youths begin fire starting they really do not understand the power of destruction that fire has, but with repeated use and experimentation, they become well-versed on those powers. It is only a matter of time before they become better acquainted with fire and choose to use it responsibly or to destroy.

Depression or anger can be at the root of some of the revenge seeking that often accompanies fire starting. Depression has feelings of hopelessness, helplessness, and anger because of the repressed feelings that manifest themselves in overt aggression. At times a youth may not be able to express their anger in an appropriate fashion, so starting a fire is very passive-aggressive. Their inability to communicate their thoughts and feelings leads them to starting a fire as a clear message of their unhappiness or frustration with the individuals they are dealing with.

Peer pressure, as silly as it may be to adults, can be a strong motivator for a youth who is fire starting. The need to be accepted within a group may consist of an initiation or a demonstration of their ability to be bad. Oftentimes the fires set in these circumstances are silliness gone wrong.

Attention is a huge motivator for the pathological fire starter. The seeing of one's destruction in the news or media fuels the desire for more attention and recognition. At times, the fires will escalate the amount of media attention. In fact, as the targets become more and more prominent, the more attention the fire starter gets in the media. Fire and police departments now routinely scan the crowds at fires and videotape the audience to see if any familiar faces are present. Many an arsonist has been caught while admiring their work, when they were later recognized by officials and apprehended.

Poor or no adult supervision results in children left to their own devices. Youths who are not monitored may set fire out of boredom, peer pressure, or just for the sake of it. The lack of parental control and monitoring allows the youth to roam free and therefore they find trouble fairly easily.

Change or crisis in the child's life may send a child into an emotional or psychological spin and the only way that the child can seem to regain a sense of control is to set a fire. Fire has been known to be hypnotizing and calming. How many times have people sat around a fireplace or campfire and just stared into the flames and achieved a Zen-like feeling of inner calmness and security?

Acting out of fear or anxiety is another strong motivator for starting a fire. It is an emotional release that brings a sense of euphoria for some youths and is better than alcohol or drugs. It is a high that cannot be explained, just a wonderful feeling of power to see something crackle and burn. The sounds and smells reduce the anxiety and fear. It is a powerful drug that is all sensory and visually stimulating.

Thrill-seeking fire starting is becoming popular on Internet sites. Sacramento Metropolitan Fire District firefighters have noticed after several incidents that teenagers are now starting fire to themselves and to property in stunts inspired by Internet videos. On Web sites such as YouTube it is very easy to find videos of teens creating flamethrowers out of Super Soaker-style water guns filled with gasoline. Other videos show teens starting fire to their own clothes and even shooting Roman candle fireworks at each other. This thrill seeking is leaving youths with multiple burns and even death in some cases. Internet sites that accept these videos need to be more vigilant in enforcement of what they will publish on these popular social network sites.

FIRE PREVENTION

Children and students should be educated that fire is not a toy but a tool. Fire is dangerous, it can kill. Supervise children at all times. Store matches and lighters in secure places out of reach of children. Check the child's bedroom and look for signs of burned items or matches. Use a "Don't Touch!" approach with children under five years old. If a child is curious then demonstrate proper and safe fire use. With younger children it is easier to educate and teach. With older fire starters you will need to evaluate the function of the fire starting, whether it is environmental or pathological. The route to treatment is very different because the function is different.

The Burn Institute provides Juvenile Fire Setter Programs. These programs work directly with the child and their family in a casual confidential starting. The program will instruct the child and their family in fire and burn prevention education and show them the consequences of playing with fire.

If you suspect a child or student of fire starting, playing with fire, or constant curiosity of fire, you should contact your local fire department, police department, school, or mental health agent to have you and your child referred to the Burn Institute Juvenile Fire Setter Program.

What does the program look like? It begins with a two-hour session at the Burn Institute with the child and at least one parent or guardian, in a casual setting. There is a confidential interview with the child and a parent or guardian present to determine the reasons for the behavior. The program components provide education on preventing fire and burns in juvenile fire starting as well as the consequences of playing with fire.

A contract between child, parent, and Burn Institute stating that fire is a tool and needs to be used carefully and responsibly is created and signed by all participants. The program is an intervention developed to help instill knowledge in children and their families on fire safety. It may not cure or stop fire play and curiosity. It is important to closely monitor children, supervise youths, and recognize the signs of fire starting.

There are also public fire safety groups once a month at the Burn Institute. It is important to check with your local fire department, police department, and local school district for other fire safety programs.

As a parent or a teacher, it is necessary to reinforce the child for choosing a positive alternative instead of behaving in an inappropriate or violent manner. One must provide the child with positive role models who use positive problem-solving techniques to resolve problems.

At times provide an outlet for the child who thinks about starting fires to express these thoughts by allowing art work, diary writing, or self-recording. As an adult let the child know you care about their feelings and thoughts. Common sense says always providing close monitoring for children is the best form of intervention.

Parents: Set a Good Example

• Install and maintain smoke alarms and fire extinguishers.
• Plan and practice fire escape drills in your home.
• Regularly inspect your home for fire hazards.
• Always use "safety sense" when making or using fire.
• Point out to your children the safety rules you and others are following throughout the day.

Parental Warning Signs

Parents need to be on the lookout for the following as well. These are the warning signs that your child may be playing with fire:
Collections of matches, lighters, or other fire tools

Aerosol cans that don't belong in a bedroom
Aerosol cans missing from other parts of the house
Gasoline or kerosene that wasn't purchased by an adult
Questions from child about what items are flammable
Clothes that smell like gasoline or fire
(Burn Institute)

Everyone in the community (parents and caregivers, the local fire and police departments, mental health counselors and social services, juvenile justice, schools, churches, medical community, youth service workers, public and private business, insurance industry, and other community leaders) should be on the lookout as well.

Teachers, Counselors, and Community Leaders: Take Responsibility for Fire Safety.

- Teach fire safety in preschool through high school programs.
- Participate in training to learn about juvenile fire starters.
- Help raise awareness in your community about juvenile fire starters.
- Know the resources in your community to help juvenile fire starters—or help develop juvenile fire starters program.

The following recommendations are promoted by FEMA as a way to educate but also to build awareness in families, schools, and the general public. It is only with education and programming can this issue be resolved. It is a totally preventative issue. It can be stopped before it begins.

What Can The Community Do?

- Prevent curiosity fire starting in the first place: provide fire safety education for children and youth throughout the year.
- Organize a coordinated, community based, screening/intervention program.
- Identify and provide for the child's and family's needs (fire safety education, counseling, social services, etc.) using community resources.
- Assist parents, caregivers, and all who work with children to better understand children's involvement with fire and when and where to go for help (FEMA, 2003).

These recommendations are realistic and doable. Communities can achieve the guidelines with an enormous amount of success if there a consistent implementation. It is only by being vigilant can communities begin addressing this issue.

Recommended Reading list for Fire starting

Aftab, Parry. *The Parent's Guide to Protecting Your Children in Cyberspace* (New York: McGraw-Hill Professional, 1999).

Bertolino, Bob. *Change-Orientated Therapy with Adolescents and Young Adults* (New York: W.W. Norton & Co., 2003).

Buckingham, Marcus, and Donald Clifton. *Now Discover Your Strengths* (New York: The Free Press, 2001). Garbarino, James. *Lost Boys: Why Our Sons Turn Violent and How We Can Save Them* New York: Free Press, 1999).

Garbarino, James. *Parents Under Siege: Why You Are the Solution, Not the Problem, in Your Child's Life* (New York: Touchstone, 2001.)

Garbarino, James. *See Jane Hit: Why Girls are Growing More Violent and What We Can Do About It* (New York: Penguin Press, 2004).

Hubble, M., B. Duncan, and S. Miller. *The Heart and Soul of Change: What Works in Therapy* (Washington D.C.: American Psychological Association, 1999).

Johnson, Simon. *Keeping Your Kids Safe on the Internet* (New York: McGraw-Hill, 2004).

Levy, R., B. O'Hanlon, and T. Goode. *Try and Make Me! Simple Strategies That Turn Off the Tantrums and Create Cooperation* (Emmaus, PA: Rodale, 2001).

Payne, Ruby K. *A Framework for Understanding Poverty* (Chicago: Aha Publications,).

Reivich, Karen and A. Shattle. *The Resilience Factor* (New York: Broadway Books, 2003).

Schwartau, Winn. *Internet and Computer Ethics for Kids (And Parents and Teachers Who Haven't A Clue* (Seminole, FL: Interpact Press, 2001).

Turnell, A. and S. Edwards. *Signs of Safety: A Solution and Safety Oriented Approach to Child Protection Casework* (New York: W.W. Norton & Co., 1999).

Wexler, David. *The Adolescent Self* (New York: W.W. Norton & Co., 1991).

Wolin, S.J., and S. Wolin. *The Resilient Self: How Survivors of Troubled Families Rise Above Adversity* (New York: Villard Press, 1993).

In conclusion, fire starting is a behavior that can be prevented. Adults in a variety of roles must be committed to providing education and awareness about what fire can and will do to possessions and people. It is extremely imperative that adults intervene at the first sign of fire use. This behavior needs to be monitored frequently and addressed with interventions that truly address the function of the fire starting. Fire starting is not a phase that will go away with age or maturity. It will be eliminated once the function of why the youth or child is starting the fires is addressed fully by interventions that lead to long-standing changes. The best solution is adult monitoring and supervision.

Chapter 5

Foster Children and the Foster System

Life circumstances for many children prevent them from having an ideal childhood. The factors involved in children becoming part of the foster care system are numerous and as varied as are the families that these children come from. These factors are often rooted in alcoholism, abuse, abandonment, poverty, mental health, and the criminal justice system. The child welfare system was created as a mechanism to provide all children with the basics of life—shelter, food, and protection. The system as it exists presently is not without its challenges.

The statistics of how many children are presently in the system vary quite considerably. "As of September 30, 2009, there were 423,773 children and youth who have found their way into the child welfare-foster care system throughout the United States." Each state has a system that is responsible for the monitoring and well-being of children and is funded by state and federal dollars. "The mean age of most children in foster care is 9.6 years of age. The average length of stay for children in foster care is 26.7 months" (AFCARS, 2010).

Where children are placed will often vary depending on the need or situation that the child is in, from a pre-adoptive home, where an individual is well-trained to provide temporary care, to foster family relative home, which often has resulted in grandparents becoming the caregiver.

Group homes that are funded and monitored by the local community agencies and are near the child's home community will be used to try to keep the child relatively close to friends, family, and school. A child may be placed in an institution, which is rare in 2011, as there are very few of these organizations still available.

Some children do require supervised independent living, which allows the parent or family to stay in touch. If the child is a runaway, there may be a series of trial home visits as a way to transition the child or youth back into the home. "The placements will depend on the child or youth's needs, both behaviorally and emotionally" (AFCARS, 2010).

One of the major goals of any foster care system in the United States and worldwide is to reunify the troubled youth with a parent or principal caretaker. One of the major components in this reunification is that there needs to be an adult who is ready and able to provide some stability and consistency in the lives of the youth. Oftentimes parents do not have the capacity and skills needed to provide the necessary staples of life and are still unable to provide a safe and caring environment where the basics are provided. This results in the child or youth having extended stays in placement.

However, when the parent or caregiver is able to provide some level of stability and consistency with a commitment to provide adequate care, this occurs approximately 49 percent of the time (AFCARS, 2010). There is a difference between youths and children who have been completely removed from any family connection and those who live with another family member or relative. The research indicated that approximately 4 percent continue to be bonded to the natural family unit, which in my opinion is very small, percentage wise. This states that 96 percent of kids taken away do not want to return to their home families. There is hope that at times the extended family is able to provide care to this 4 percent, and the child welfare system does see this as a well-received and optimal solution for many troubled children (AFCARS, 2010).

Getting children out of foster care and into an adopted home is a goal that the child welfare system strives to achieve. Children and youth want to feel safe and protected so that the relationship that occurs between foster parent and foster child is one of emotional and physical bonding that is created out of adversity. These children want to feel a sense of belonging to someone.

Many foster children want to be adopted so that they can belong to someone and not be carted from one group home or placement and have an overwhelming sense of being lost. Adoption is often a faraway dream that is never a reality for many. This process is difficult and very time-consuming, often with a battle between the natural parents and foster parents. The courts have often returned the children to their natural parents, to the chagrin of the adoptive parents who want to provide a safe and nurturing home for these youths who are often riddled with issues. Approximately only 2 percent of foster children ever get adopted (AFCARS, 2010).

The reality is that many children and youth end up in long-term foster care, emancipation, and long-term guardianship where they live out their adolescent years wishing and hoping to be free at eighteen, when they can escape. Often the escape is ultimately more dangerous than the placement or home, where they would have been part of a family unit.

"The gender of children in foster care is fairly predictable and equally divided between boys being about 53% and girls 47%" (AFCARS, 2010). These statistics do vary from year to year but stay very consistent. "Race and ethnicity of children in foster care is spread out, with approximately 30% African American, 40% Caucasian, and 20% Hispanics, while the remaining number is divided among other races. Asians compose the lowest number of children in foster care" (AFCARS,2010). These statistics bring up some interesting questions as to why some cultures are more likely to access the foster care system than others. The answers I believe are in the lack of family values, connections, support within the family unit, and pride in the community.

"Looking at how many children exited foster care in 2009; approximately 276,266 were able to be discharged. This left 147,507 who were still within the system. The average age was 9.6 years. Reasons for exiting the foster care system were reunification with parents (51%), living with a relative (8%), adoption (20%), emancipation (11%), and guardianship (7%), with the remaining children either runaways or transferred to another agency." The length of stay in foster care for these children was 22 months overall, before being discharged (AFCARS, 2010).

"The age that children seem to enter into foster care is around 5 years of age, which seems to parallel their entry into the school system. It is noteworthy that parents up to this time seem to be able to manage under the radar of the child welfare system, without being identified. "Approximately 69,000 parents had their rights terminated in 2009. The process from entry of child to termination of parental rights takes about 24.7 months" (AFCARS 2010). This termination of rights is for a multiple of reasons (abuse, neglect, abandonment, etc.).

When investigating the gender of foster children who are adopted it seems to be fairly close in terms of gender, approximately 51 percent of the males and 49 percent of the females (AFCARS, 2010). "The average age for adoption is 6.3 years of age. The ethnicities of the children who are adopted are 44% White, 25% Black, and 21% Hispanic. The people who adopted foster care children are 66% married couples, 28% single females, 2% unmarried couples, and 3% single males" (AFCARS, 2010).

"The largest majority of the people who adopt are foster parents 54%, a child's relative is 32% and non-relatives are 14%" (AFCARS, 2010). It is encouraging to see that people who do provide foster care do build relationships with these children and youth and do end up adopting them, which hopefully provides them with a secure environment.

There are a number of steps that potential foster parents must take in order to become a foster parent. Each state completes their process a little differently, but generally, each state will have similar requirements. Some requirements to become a foster parent may be:

Background check and fingerprinting
Comprehensive home study to ensure child safety
Classroom hours
First-aid certification
Medical clearances for all adults and children currently in the home
Statement proclaiming that corporal punishment will not be used
Statement advising your role as a mandated reporter
(AFCARS, 2010)

The goal in finding suitable foster parents is the primary focus of many of the agencies throughout the country. The reality is that there are more children than suitable placements.

How does one measure the impact of being in the foster care system? The impact of being in foster care often leads to much more psychological dysfunction and more acting out as compared to children who are in the same gender or age group. In a study of adults who were in foster care in several states, they were found to have double the incidence of depression—20 percent as compared to 10 percent (Wikipedia.org/foster care).

Foster children have a higher rate of post-traumatic stress disorder (PTSD) because of the ongoing challenges of being moved from one place to another. They are often uprooted and are unable to form lasting bonds with the people who are their caregivers. "Children in foster care have a higher probability of having Attention Deficit Hyperactivity Disorder, deficits in executive functioning, anxiety, and other developmental problems" (Wikipedia.org). These children will often experience higher degrees of incarceration and, at a much earlier age, poverty due to the fact that they have no ability to gain employment often due to their age, homelessness because of having run away, and suicide because of the feelings of hopelessness and helplessness. Recent studies in the United States suggest that many foster care placements in many states are more detrimental to children than remaining in a troubled home (Wikipedia.org/foster Care). The system that is charged with their care and support ends up being the thing that destroys them psychologically and physically. What a sad fact this is!

It has been shown repeatedly that children who enter the foster care system have issues in neurodevelopment and development overall. Many of the children who enter foster care do so at approximately 5 years of age. The processes that govern the development of personality traits, stress response, and cognitive skills are formed during this period.

The developing brain of a child is directly influenced by negative environmental factors. Children in troubled homes often are not exposed to a variety of learning experiences and will not get the type of stimulation that is needed for active brain development. The reason for this lack of neurodevelopment is often due to emotional neglect, poor nutrition, exposure to violence in the home environment, and child abuse, which can include physical, sexual, and emotional abuse.

During the most critical time of their development, children are experiencing some of the most horrific experiences of their young lives. These early years impact their academic and school development—approximately 75 percent of foster children drop out of high school (Wikipedia.org).

Children in foster care have a higher incidence of post-traumatic stress disorder (PTSD). "In one study (Dubner and Motta, 1999), 60% of children in foster care who had experienced sexual abuse had PTSD and 42% of those who had been physically abused fulfilled the PTSD criteria. PTSD was also found in 18% of the children who were not abused" (Wikipedia.org).

These statistics do indicate that there is a major impact in being in the foster care system, as many are removed from their homes because of the sexual or physical abuse. Even though the child may seem fine on the outside, what is going on internally and emotionally, however, is a chaotic storm of emotions that often will lead to acting out behaviors that are both dangerous and lethal, in some cases, as they are unable to control this avalanche of emotions.

Foster children are at an increased risk for a variety of eating disorders, in comparison to the general population, because of the use of food as an emotional support. "Obese children in foster care are more prone to becoming further overweight and obese, and in a study done in the United Kingdom, 35% of foster children experienced an increase in Body Mass Index (BMI) once in care" (Hadfield, 2008). This speaks to the lack of proper nutrition in foster homes and to the use of food to control or suppress some of the emotional impact of being placed in a foster home.

Foster children have been found to suffer from Hyperphagic Short Stature syndrome (HSS). This syndrome is not common and is often represented as a condition that is characterized by short stature (being small overall for one's age) due to insufficient growth hormone production, an excessive appetite (hyperphagia), and mild learning disabilities (Wikipedia.org/ foster_care).

There is very little research that has proven the existence of a genetic component. HSS is triggered by being exposed to an environment of high psychosocial stress, and it is not uncommon in children in foster homes or other stressful environments. HSS seems to improve once the child is removed from the stressful environment (Gilmour, 2001, Skuse 1996, Demb 1991).

Food Maintenance Syndrome is characterized by a set of unhealthy, even pathological behaviors around food intake, and the relationship that the child has with food. This syndrome is very frequently observed in foster care placements. The reasons are multiple as to why it exists. It can be from lack of availability to nutritious food or the irregular shopping practices of the foster care parent. When observing this syndrome one looks for a pattern of excessive eating and food acquisition and resembles "the behavioral correlates of Hyperphagic Short Stature." It is hypothesized that this syndrome is triggered by the stress and maltreatment foster children are subjected to—it was prevalent amongst 25 percent of the study group in New Zealand (Tarren-Sweeney 2006).

Bulimia Nervosa is seven times more prevalent among former foster children than in the general population (Wikipedia.org/fostercare). The fact that bulimia is so present speaks volumes to the fact that children in foster care are not receiving the type of emotional support to deal with their issues and therefore resort to food as a way to comfort themselves from their troubled lives. Children needing psychological interventions while in foster care often go without and resort to a variety of less-than-desirable interventions that lead to additional mental health issues. The eating disorders just get piled on to the list of other comorbid factors.

The number of children who have long-lasting psychological and emotional issues due to foster care experiences are too numerous to count. Many of these children because of the abuse are up to seven times more likely than their same-aged peers to be abused. This indicates that very few foster children escape the reality of abuse. Children who have experienced maltreatment are also at risk of having psychiatric problems such as depression, anxiety, attachment disorders, dissociative problems, and acting out symptoms.

It has been reported that three out of ten of the homeless in the United States are former foster children (V. Roman, 1995). This indicates a failure in the foster care system to adequately prepare these children with skills that will enable them to become productive citizens once they reach adulthood.

According to a study done by the Casey Family Study of foster care alumni, up to 80 percent are doing poorly, with a quarter to a third of former foster children at or below the poverty line (Wikipedia.org). Something is not working within the system to create a whole quarter of this population that ends up on the street after they turn 18. This is three times the national poverty rate. This is a problem that needs to be addressed immediately by the services that give these foster care children skills and education to prevent becoming homeless. Children and youth who are homeless had multiple placements as children and were found to have been moved frequently and were unable to establish any types of roots in one location. This roaming existence lends itself to becoming adaptable and can easily continue this lifestyle as a young adult.

Is it possible to predict whether an individual with a history of foster care will become homeless at an earlier age? The answer is yes. There are a series of predictors that indicate that if a child or youth has had a history of being in the foster care system, the length of time of being in those placements will indicate a higher possibility of homelessness. "Caucasians who become homeless are more likely to have a history of foster care than Hispanics or African Americans. The length of time a person remains homeless is prolonged in individuals who were in foster care" (Roman and Wolfe 1995).

An unfortunate and realistic statistic is that nearly half of foster children in the United States become homeless when they turn 18. These youths are often released by the state without the proper training or education or employment to sustain themselves in productive ways. The solution would be that hopefully most foster care children are placed in adoptive homes where they have a family connection or an emotional support system. "One of every 10 foster children stays in foster care longer than seven years, and each year about 15,000 reach the age of majority and leave foster care without a permanent family—many to join the ranks of the homeless or to commit crimes and be imprisoned" (Lyons-Ruth 1999; Greenberg 1999).

According to a nationwide study of runaway youths, more than one-third had been in foster care in the year before they took to the streets. "More than one out of five youths who arrive at a shelter come directly from a foster or group home, with 38 percent nationally saying they had been in foster care at some time during the previous year, the study found" (Lyons-Ruth 1999; Greenberg 1999).

"In a new phenomenon, almost 11 percent of youths said they were homeless and living on the streets before coming to shelters." These findings were the most disturbing to emerge from a study of 170 runaway shelters (Los Angeles Times, 1992). This was quoted from 1992, yet the numbers in 2010 have increased through the roof. Some experts estimate that 45 percent of those leaving foster care become homeless within a year (San Diego Daily, October 1996). A California study in Contra Costa County found that a third of children placed in foster care eventually end up homeless, and 35 percent are arrested while in foster care (R. Thoma 1996, www.liftingtheveil.org).

What are the causes of such statistics? Inappropriate placements and a lack of needed services are partly to blame. "Children are put in inappropriate placements, not designed to offer family counseling, psychiatric treatment, or drug treatment. Children are not prepared to return to families, nor are they provided with a specialized educational and vocational training they need to survive after they become 18. As a result, they become the new homeless"

(Dennis Lepak). Dennis made this point back in 1988, and unfortunately it is still very true in 2010. Why has the system been so slow to change? Why is it so resistant? Is it all about money and resources, or about a system that sees these kids as throwaways and is not willing to invest in them?

The problem is universal in scope. The child welfare system and the government of human services' lack of commitment to foster care are helping create a population of throwaway children, many of whom go on to lives of substance abuse, homelessness, and crime.

Federal funding contributes to the crisis, as Eileen McCaffrey, executive director of the Orphan Foundation of America, explains: "Since federal funding guidelines encourage state-run foster care programs to emphasize short-term, crisis-management services, nongovernment players must concentrate on longer-range, skill-development programs. Youngsters leaving foster-care ill-equipped for life on their own often end up homeless or permanently dependent on welfare services" (Eileen McCaffrey, 1994). It looks like nothing has changed since 1994. We are still at the same place with state-run funding and resource management. It is incredibly sad!

Even among the homeless, the risks of continued family disruption are significantly greater than among the general population. An ongoing study by the Institute for Children and Poverty reveals "that homeless families whose heads of households grew up in foster care are at greatest risk of dissolution. Individuals who grew up in foster care are 30% more likely to be substance abusers and 50% more likely to have a history of domestic violence than the overall homeless population. Twice as many of these heads of households have already lost at least one child to foster care" (Institute for Children and Poverty, 1998).

Several federal studies in the 1990s of former foster care wards found "that one-fourth had been homeless, 40% were on public assistance and half were unemployed. Connecticut officials estimate 75% of youths in the state's criminal justice system were once in foster care" (Bayles and Cohen, 1995). According to a survey by the National Association of Social Workers, "20% of children living in runaway shelters come directly from foster care. Children placed in out-of-home care, *regardless of the reason*, are at higher risk of developing alcohol and drug problems. The survey also found that 80% of prisoners in Illinois spent time in foster care as children" (Beth Azar, 1995).

Karl Dennis, executive director of the Illinois-based Kaleidoscope, the first child welfare agency in the country to provide unconditional care for children, says that in California, 80 percent of the adults in the correctional facilities "are graduates of the state, the juvenile justice, the child welfare, the mental health and the special education systems."

Children and youth in foster care are more likely to attempt and succeed at suicide. They also have a higher rate of mortality at a young age than their same-aged peers. They are more likely to die due to accidents, suicide, substance abuse, and illness. Since so many end up on the street, they contract life-threatening diseases, including HIV and AIDS.

"In 2004, the Pew Commission on Children in Foster Care issued its recommendations for overhauling and improving the nation's safety net for vulnerable children. As of December 2008, many of the financing recommendations issued by the Pew Commission have been enacted via the Fostering Connections to Success and Increasing Adoptions Act (H.R. 6893), and all of the court reforms are well underway in every state throughout the nation" (www.kidsarewaitingorg/assets/docs/PL%20110–351%20Summary). This was a step in the right direction to begin improving the fate of many of the foster kids who live in every state.

Signed into law by President George W. Bush on October 7, 2008, Public Law 110–351 had as its mandate to "improve the lives of children and youth in foster care and increase the likelihood that they will be able to leave the foster care system to live permanently with relative guardians or adoptive families." "The law tries to accomplish this by extending and providing services for relatives, children in foster care, tribal nations, and adoptive families" (www.kidsarewaiting.org/assets/docs/PL%20110–351%20Summary).

What does the law do for children currently in foster care? There are five areas that have been noted as having positive outcomes for these youths:

1. Extends federal partnership of youth in foster care to age 21
2. Better prepares youth to leave foster care
3. Better educational outcomes
4. Better health outcomes
5. More siblings together
   (www.kidsarewaiting.org/assets/docs/PL%20110–351%20Summary)

It extends federal partnership of youth in foster care to age twenty-one. There is now accountability between states and the federal government. Youths are not set adrift once they turn eighteen as in the past. If they need to, they are still able to access services, supports, and psychological interventions.

States have the option to use federal funds to continue services and supports to older youth in foster care, guardianships, and adoptions until age twenty-one. The law better prepares youth to leave foster care. They now require each state to develop a personalized services plan for older youth leaving foster care.

There are now better educational outcomes for these youths. The law requires each state to ensure that children in foster care are enrolled full-time in school and improve their educational stability. The fact that they will have access to schooling and possible vocational training will enable them to go out and find a job that will sustain them and enable them to have a regular life.

These youths now have better health outcomes as it requires each state to develop a statewide plan to improve oversight and coordination of health services provided to children in foster care. Many of these youths do not have the income or employment to access healthcare and very few have insurance so this will enable them to seek out help when they need it.

On a positive note many more siblings are together. Each state is required to make reasonable efforts to place siblings removed from their home in the same foster care or adoptive setting, unless doing so would be against their best interests.

A mother's personal story:

I first met my oldest son when he was 3 and 1/2. Malnourished, bottle-rot front teeth, hair unkempt and unwashed. He'd never had a real haircut, had never had an immunization, (never had) a birthday party or portrait taken. He met me, across the teacher's desk from where he stood, asking for a piece of candy from my candy jar. I was 31, a new mother, and immediately fell in love with this boy who asked me to take him home and be his mom. A victim of a drug-addicted mother, heroin-addicted grandmother, and abandoned in a homeless shelter at age 3 1/2 with his infant sister. Left to be raised by his maternal aunt who had never been off welfare. Six months later, he was abandoned again, this time to foster care. He had his first birthday party ever, in our home, as our foster child, at age 5.

Five years later we, my husband and I have mastered terminology such as attachment disorder, suicidal ideology, childhood onset bipolar, attention deficit disorder, Post Traumatic Stress Disorder, psychotropic medication, and Fetal Alcohol Syndrome to name a few. Our son, whom we adopted at age 7, now resides in a treatment facility for emotionally disturbed boys. Our family has experienced grief beyond measure, severance of family ties due to my son's behavior and our subsequent responses.

You see, we are also parenting our two birth children, along with my son's younger birth sister. We have been told by our state adoption agency that we have been allotted 18 months of services for my son, at that time, we will need to bring him home; ready or not. My son and his sister have 7 other KNOWN siblings, all in similar situations. What about their rights?

(An Adopted Mother's Grief retrieved from library.adoption.com/articles/an-adoptive-mothers-grief.html).

The following is a list of possible resources to inform your practices or education around the issue of children in foster care. This list is not exhaustive but is provided as a resource to begin the discussion or fact- finding journey to help individuals who may be suffering or are caught in the web of the foster care system. This list is provided as references only and this author does not recommend one program over another.

1. The Arrow Project
   A comprehensive and integrated social service agency providing quality care to children and families in the States of Texas and Maryland. Currently the largest treatment foster care provider in Texas. Operates Arrow Center for Education and Arrow Diagnostic Center in Baltimore, Maryland.
2. Bakersfield Foster Care Resource
   Kern County's local foster family agency, it provides adoption services for children previously destined for long-term foster care. They also operate a group home for severely emotionally disturbed boys and provide CEUs for childcare professionals.
3. Boys' Village
   Has an innovative network model for treatment foster care that empowers foster parents to work with very troubled kids.
4. Defran Systems
   Provides total software solutions for your foster care agency.
5. The Foster Circle
   Foster-related information exchange and support channel provider.
6. FosterCareAgency.Org
   Information for foster parents, get a pen pal, moderated help section, difficult behavior problems, articles, forms, database of agencies, agencies online, links, manual, regulations, connect with other foster parents, newsletter, real life stories, poems, online training, and much more.
7. Family Finders
   Family Finders is a coalition of social service agencies contracted with Alabama Department of Human Resources to recruit and train foster and adoptive parents.
8. Foster and Adoptive Parents Association of Oneida County, Inc.
   They are a nonprofit foster and adoptive parent association which provides information, training, and support to foster and adoptive parents. They also have a listing of children available for adoption on the website.
9. Foster_Moms_n_Dads
   A site where foster parents can provide each other with the support, through mailings, via phone or even personal contact. There is a lack of support out there, so join us and we will have unity and knowledge with our numbers.

10. Foster Parent Allegations
    False Allegations . . . the Dark Side of Foster Care. Allegations occur
    daily across the country, yet no one tells you what you will encounter
    when you are accused.
11. Foster Parents CARE
    A nonprofit, charitable organization dedicated to the success of all chil-
    dren worldwide. It is the first Foster Parents Association dedicated en-
    tirely to the Internet community. It is a wonderful, huge, interactive site
    for foster parents and everyone involved in foster care.
12. Foster Parent Community
    The Foster Parent Community is brought to you by Barbara Leiner. A
    great site, don't miss it! You will want to add a bookmark for this site.
    You will find stories, poems, and activities for children, as well as legal
    information.
13. FosterParentTraining.com
    Online training for new and licensed foster parents.
14. Hannah and Her Mama: Older Child Adoption
    Older child adoption resources. Articles, parenting tips, links, books, and
    more. Appropriate for both adoptive and foster families.
15. Life Book
    A book suitable for recording and preserving memories as well as medi-
    cal information for any age child. Additional pages for photos and inter-
    national versions.
16. Lutheran Social Services of the South, Inc.
    Our services include basic foster care and therapeutic foster care. We
    provide quality, supportive and professional services to foster children
    and foster families. Our services include basic foster care and therapeutic
    foster care.
17. Megilligan's Island
    Providing foster care and special needs adoption information in the Cen-
    tral Kentucky area.
18. National Youth Advocate Program
    The National Youth Advocate Program, Inc. has affiliates in Ohio, West
    Virginia, Illinois, Indiana, South Carolina, and Georgia and provides
    traditional and therapeutic foster care, emergency shelter care, diag-
    nostic and treatment services, and in-home services to youth and their
    families.
19. North Carolina Foster Parents Association
    The NCFPA Web Page offers information for foster, adoptive, and kinship
    parents. Caregivers can find information, training, education, technical as-
    sistance, and support. Also, foster parents can sign up for the fall Conference

in Durham and select the workshops they want to attend via this web page, and send in the registration and cost of the workshops selected.

20. Oakland Family Services

    Oakland Family Services is a private, nonprofit, human service organization. Since 1921, OFS has been dedicated to strengthening families by providing quality treatment, education, and prevention services throughout southeastern Michigan.

21. Parent Consultation Services

    Informative, educational, Book, booklet, resources, parent training, join the association, good information.

22. Professional Tutors of America

    Provide tutoring services for foster children in California, Nevada, and Arizona.

23. The Quality Improvement Network

    The Quality Improvement Network links Quality Improvement/Quality Assurance departments from Foster care agencies to share information and resources.

24. Texas State Foster Parents, Inc.

    Advocating for foster parents and children in the state of Texas.

25. A World for Children

    A Texas-based Child Placing agency dedicated to "Changing the world . . . one child at a time." Foster Parent services, Emergency Placements, Assessment Center.

    This list of resources is but a small sample of what is available. There is more information on all aspects of Adoptions and Foster care at ABCAdoptions.com. This website is plethora of ideas and suggestions for increasing one's knowledge on this topic.

Foster children have rights. However, many individuals who become foster parents do not know that these children and youth have a series of rights. The comprehensive list below is for adult awareness. This information was taken directly from the website Know Your Rights. This list was kept in its entirety and is to be used as a benchmark to assure that children in the foster care system are informed and that their rights are respected.

Youth have the Right to Live In a Safe, Comfortable Home with:

• enough clothes and healthy food
• own place to store their things
• an allowance (if in a group home)

- a phone that can be used to make confidential calls (unless a judge says you cannot)

Youth have the Right to:

- be treated with respect
- go to religious services and activities of their choice, and send and get unopened mail (unless a judge says someone else can open mail)
- contact people who are not in the foster care system (like friends, church members, teachers, and others)
- make contact with social workers, attorneys, probation officers, CASAs, foster youth advocates and supporters, or anyone else involved with case
- be told about placement by social worker or probation officer

No One Can:

- lock them in a room or building (unless in a community treatment facility)
- abuse physically, sexually, or emotionally for any reason
- punish by physically hurting for any reason
- look through things unless they have a good and legal reason

Connection with a Caring Adult:

- Youth have the right to identify and maintain relationships with appropriate people who are important to them, as long as it's in their best interest. The intent of current law is that no child shall leave foster care without a permanent, caring relationship with an adult. Talk to a social worker or attorney about who is important to the youth.

Youth have Rights at Court Too. Youth Can:

- go to court and talk to the judge
- see and get a copy of their court report and their case plan
- keep court records private, unless the law says otherwise
- be told by social worker or probation officer and attorney about any changes in case plan or placement

Youth have Health Rights. Youth Can:

- see a doctor, dentist, eye doctor, or talk to a counselor if need to
- refuse to take medicines, vitamins, or herbs (unless a doctor or judge says youth must)

Youth have School Rights. Youth Can:

- go to school every day
- go to after-school activities right for age and developmental level

Youth have the Right to Do Some Things on Their Own. Youth Can:

- have their own emancipation bank account (unless case plan says you cannot)
- learn job skills right for their age
- work, unless the law says youth are too young to manage the money they earn (if right for your age, developmental level, and it's in case plan)
- go to Independent Living Program classes and activities if old enough

Youth have Family Rights Too. Youth Can:

- visit and contact their brothers and sisters (unless a judge says you cannot)
- contact parents and other family members, too (unless a judge says you cannot)

Youth have Other Rights Too. Youth Can:

- tell the judge how feel about your family, lawyer, and social worker
- tell the judge what want to happen in case
- have their own lawyer
- live with a family member if that would be a safe place
- call the Foster Care Ombudsman Office and Community Care Licensing at any time
- get help with school if they need it

YOUTH CAN PARTICIPATE IN SOCIAL ACTIVITIES

Youth have the right to participate in age-appropriate extracurricular, enrichment, and social activities such as church, school and community activities, sleepovers with friends, and scouting and 4-H, without requiring criminal background checks of chaperones, friends, and friends' parents or supervisors (Know Your Rights, 2010). These rights are needed so as to be able to protect all foster children from experiencing abuse or trauma at the hands of foster parents or the foster system.

Below is a personal story of a young man's journey in the Foster Care system. Dan has given permission to use his story as a way to build understanding from a first person perspective. His hope is that when you read his story that you will become more sensitive to the issues, concerns, and tribulations that a kid in foster care may experience in their lives on a daily basis. His story is meant to teach and touch you in a very personal way.

DAN'S STORY: I entered foster care when I was five years old, roughly 1990. My dad was an abusive alcoholic. He often abused my mom, but later abused my sister and I. So, because of that . . . I entered foster care in California first. It was like a night thing. Because along with the abuse we were also living on the streets, going from Salvation Army to wherever we could find a place to live, to living in the car and we didn't have money.

Someone called us in and took my sister and I away for at least for a night so my dad or my mom was able to get some sort of funding, so they were able to support us a little bit. I stayed in a foster home in California for one night and then we were transferred, my sister and I were transferred into this orphanage place where there was lots of kids in the same predicament as we were. Some were there for about a year some were there for a couple of nights. My sister and I were there for a couple of nights. That was our first stint. My family moved down to Florida and that's where a lot of my experiences with foster care were, mainly negative.

My dad continued with his alcoholism and continued with his abuse. He abused my mom, abused my sister, abused me. We were, again, homeless, living wherever we could find a place near library roofs, like the overhangs, random peoples' houses, occasionally a hotel, finally in a car. Some lady reported my parents to what's called HRS, which was near Keystone, Keystone Heights, Florida. At that agency, it's like social workers they took us, my sister and I away from my parents. My parents lost custody, this was about 1991 and we were brought to the Wheelers. They were our second official foster home. We stayed there for a good amount of time. I was in kindergarten, and first grade.

I was going to school as a foster kid, especially at that young of age I was a troubled kid. I didn't have much structure, but teachers did not have confidence in us, or especially in me. They labeled me as a troubled kid. I was often sent to detention, never really given the choice to excel. They all told me I won't succeed and I won't make it out of high school, I would be in jail, the whole nine yards. That aggravated me a while and that's probably what motivated me for the past 20 something years to be where I am today.

Having teachers especially when I started going to school as a foster kid, just starting right off going to school going to kindergarten, first grade, second grade third grade, teachers were all telling me the same thing, I will not succeed, I will not make a difference, I will be in jail, I will be in a gang. It's not the best hearing that from teachers who are supposed to support you and the foster families that I live with didn't support either because they are either abusive themselves, there for the funding, or just didn't care so we are kind of like outcasts.

When it comes to me and my sister going to school we have it tough from the school and we have it tough at home, which we couldn't really call home. We were often going from one foster family to another because they were sick of us or we had to leave or they had more foster kids coming in. It was like, I tell all my friends back in Florida that we were like bouncy balls, like the beach balls that you see bouncing back and forth back and forth. It's not fun because there is no stability. You're often asking what's wrong with you. You don't get that love, that nourishment and you constantly have to watch your back. There's pretty much no hope. My sister and I had to deal with that from 1991 to 1994–95.

In 1992 my mom left. I haven't seen her for 18 years, but recently talked to her a couple months ago, which was astonishing, it was amazing. My dad tried to get custody of us again. It didn't work out. He was more abusive; he was more of an alcoholic. He actually stuck a fork in my hand. I am a very protective person, especially when it comes to my sister, especially if someone takes food away from my sister, I was going to protect her and dad stuck a fork in my hand.

There would be other times when dad, when no one listened to him, or if the kids wouldn't listen to him he would beat us up. We often experienced that when we did live with our parents or my dad mainly because my mom left and we experienced that as foster kids too. I'd get beat up either by foster kids and foster parents. I had to experience both verbal and physical abuse by the foster parents. I had a lot of anger. I often got into trouble at school.

Then in 1995 I was sent to my grandparents up in Claremont as they decided to take custody of us. We weren't technically adopted by our grandparents, we were just there. I don't really call them foster parents, just in that whole situation where they took us in; it was as bad as living at a foster home. I was not allowed to have friends over; there was no social life, similar to living in a foster home. I was allowed one shower a week. I had to wear the same clothes. If I didn't do what I was told I would go without eating for a while. If I had an argument or dispute my grandfather and I would get into a tussle and I would usually end up having to go back upstairs as punishment. It was the same thing that I experienced in Florida, if I didn't do something I would get sent to my room.

The thing about foster homes is that when foster families have their own kids they will nurture those kids. When they have these foster kids come in the foster kids were like hand me downs, second hand, unimportant, they are just there. It's that lack of connection building, we were just there, we were just taking up space.

In 2000 I would have to say the most positive foster home experience happened. I decided to take matters into my own hands with my grandparents. For a while the abuse was getting so much that when I was in 7th grade I almost committed suicide because it was so much. I deal with Post Traumatic Stress Disorder and I have to deal with all that stuff going in my head, and in 7th grade it was getting too much, I saw a lot of counseling for that.

In 2000 I had enough. It was 8th grade, I called DCYF. I had a meeting with both the social workers and they brought my case to the district court and they took me out immediately. They left my sister there because they didn't have enough evidence for my sister to be taken out. I lived over with my foster mom Cathy, which was awesome. I got to live with my best friend. It was probably the most positive experience I've had living in a foster home. They taught me a lot of life skills. There was no neglect, no abuse.

There was some tension because I wasn't their kid so it was often uncomfortable. I don't like calling someone mom, I don't like calling someone dad, because I don't have that connection. I was able to experience life. They were very positive, very supportive, things I've never felt before. "Dan, you can do this, you can go to college, you will go to college," instead of "Dan you will be in a gang, you will drop out of high school and end up dying, being dead because you are a troubled kid."

It was a total 180 degree change that I had never experienced before and because of them I am in college. I actually almost developed straight A's, in my classes which I never had when I was in Florida. I was labeled with being special needs, I never consider myself that anymore because I had more confidence for who I was and I wanted to build from that, but I also wanted to prove people wrong. I always disliked when teachers, foster parents would tell me that I will not make it anywhere in life. It was very discouraging. I think that's probably why a lot of the foster kids today don't do well in school because teachers don't understand where they are coming from.

Foster kids have to deal with a lot. They have a lot on their plate. In their mind there is always the thoughts "What's up with their parents, are they going to come back? Why am I going back to this foster home that continually beats me or has no care for me?"

Teachers that I have come across in Florida, even in my early elementary school years here in New Hampshire, are not supportive, they do not understand. And it's very disheartening. I think that shows in the numbers of the lack of kids who are succeeding who are foster kids.

The positive memories are there but few. I am so grateful that I was given the chance to live with this foster home from 2000–2005. It was a great experience. They made me believe in myself, which is the biggest thing; I think every child should have . . . the experience to believe in themselves.

After ten years -fifteen years of being told that I am crap, being told I could be president, that's a big thing. I definitely think the foster care system needs to be worked on and parents who think they want to become foster parents have to consider what their motives are. It sickens me that these parents who are applying to be foster parents are in it for the money, there is a lot of money. Some would take the money and buy for their leisurely use. It is sickening that way it shouldn't be about the money.

It should be about helping these kids, until they are going back to a safer home. You're supposed to give them a safe place to stay and the love and nourishment as if they were your own kids. That's your role as a foster parent. Not treating them as a black sheep and just throwing them out, that type of thing. Parents who want to be in that role, it's a lot of responsibility.

Kids are definitely troubled. I had to go through a lot of counseling. I almost went to a psych ward twice. I have been on countless meds. If it weren't for my recent foster family, I probably wouldn't have made it. I was in a gang for like three days, but I was smart enough to get out. During the sixth-seventh grade time, I just didn't care, I just started collapsing.

There are good foster families out there. I don't want to put that down, but there's a good majority who aren't. Teachers have to realize, I think the whole school system has to realize that it's not easy to be in our shoes. Another thing about foster kids, my own experience and my sister's caused her and I to deal with pretty much the same thing.

I get really jealous when I see a son, dad, mother, daughter, being together, having a good time. I never experienced that. It is something I will miss and will continue to miss for the rest of my life, until I have kids. I often wonder how will things be like, how to become a dad. What kind of traits will I have. I never had a father figure. It's these simple things, you might think it's simple, but they are monumental. What kind of person am I going to be, am I going to fall. How am I going to balance a checkbook? How am I going to pay for mortgage? Things that parents should help you with, life skills I never had that chance, or the bonding.

When it comes to holding a kid, I don't know how to react. It's sad, but I feel uncomfortable. I feel uncomfortable around families, I feel uncomfortable being close to people because I never had that closeness. Yes, I have been in relationships and stuff like that, but I hold back because I am too afraid to get close.

Being a foster kid, that's the biggest thing. We don't know who to trust, we don't know who to believe, we think the world is against us, it's very troublesome. The only other thing I have to say for teachers, especially because I am going to be one, is be mindful. If a kid looks like he is in trouble, talk to him, don't put him down, because if you are taking the time to put him down, you shouldn't be a teacher.

Interventions that may work for children in the foster system are as varied as the children, a disclaimer is offered here as each individual child has unique needs and developmental deficits. These ideas are offered as suggestions. As a caring adult, teacher, foster parent, it does not matter what your role is; become aware of children's development stages and reactions to loss. These developmental deficits may provide the answers to many of the emotional and behavioral responses especially during time of transition and stress.

Because so many children have experienced loss you need to become aware of grief responses, that is, denial, anger, guilt, and so on These are often common responses to environmental factors and stressors. They are feeling the emotions, anger and frustration but do not have a point of reference or an awareness of why it is happening.

Listen, listen, listen to children. Observe their behavior and timber of their voices. Be alert for word clues that may reflect their fears, concerns and feelings of guilt. Listen with sensitivity. Answer the feelings behind the expressions and not the expressions themselves. Expressions are like the fever of the soul, which always points to a deeper problem. It's important to find out what the child wants to talk about, and let him/her guide the conversation.

To give direction to anyone, you must first find out what direction they are presently going. Honesty is necessary and simplicity is valuable. We need to not tell all the truth at one time, but always tell the truth. Children and youth will be even more untrusting and skeptical of adult behaviors and intentions. The goal is to build trust and openness.

Never belittle the problem/feelings or minimize its seriousness for the sake of false reassurance. Integrity in this area will help build a trust relationship in which healing can take place. At times adults have great intentions to protect, but by lying or omitting key components will only backfire later in life.

Don't relax discipline on the child because of his/her situation. Boundaries and structure create an atmosphere of safety even when the boundaries and structure are resisted. The consistency of the adult behavior will model for the child what is acceptable and normal. It will provide the individual with the opportunity to see positive problem solving in action followed by excellent communication between people.

All of us who have grown up in a family structure know that there is never 100 percent compliance and agreement on all issues. Allow room for friction. Express love and affection verbally and physically. Be willing to say, "I don't know." It is okay to express that extra time and effort is needed to find answers or investigate further.

Don't make promises you can't keep later just to make the child feel better temporarily. You need to realize that these children have been lied to frequently in their early years and have developed a mistrust of adult words and behaviors. Prove to these children that you are a man or woman of integrity, that you talk the talk and walk the walk. It is by watching you they can learn new patterns of behaviors. Make yourself available, wherever you are, be all there!

Always hold out hope. Life is not easy for these children and youths. They have gotten off to a rough and rotten start. They have not been given the opportunities for love, education, home and personal development that many of their peers have gotten. The fact that they have had horrible experiences does not prevent them from having a quality of life under your guidance. The vast majority of these children want to be loved, the simple desire. They want to belong and be accepted. Is that so hard? I think we can find the energy, the resources and the internal fortitude to save these children. It is our duty.

In conclusion, the journey that Dan has lived has been repeated thousands of times with many horrible consequences and traumatic life events to these foster children. We need to protect all children no matter what. The resources and services have to be there. These services need to be efficient and offered in a timely way. We cannot afford to lose another life to the foster care system. These tragedies must stop!

Chapter 6

Substance Abuse

Drugs and Alcohol

Children at risk seem to gravitate toward substance and alcohol abuse. These substances are like a magnet. They become an integral part of these teenagers' lives. Many become addicted or frequent users.

- Every day, on average, 11,318 American youth (12 to 20 years of age) try alcohol for the first time.
- Alcoholism is a leading cause of death in adolescences relating to motor vehicle crashes, other traumatic injuries, suicide, date rape, and family and school problems.
- Young people who begin drinking before age 15 are four times more likely to develop alcoholism than those who begin drinking at 21.
- Nearly one-third (31.5 percent) of all high school students reported hazardous drinking (5-plus drinks in one setting) during the 30 days preceding the survey.
(J. Bruzzese 2007)

So what is alcohol abuse? Alcohol abuse, as described in the DSM-IV, is a psychiatric diagnosis describing the recurring use of alcoholic beverages despite negative consequences.

Physical Characteristics

- Fatigue
- Repeated health complaints
- Frequent flu-like episodes, chest pains, "allergy" symptoms, chronic cough

- Red and glazed eyes
- Impaired ability to fight off common infections and fatigue
- Impaired short-term memory
- Change in health or grooming

Emotional Characteristics

- Personality change
- Sudden mood changes
- Irritability, anger, and hostility
- Irresponsible behavior
- Low self-esteem
- Poor judgment
- Feelings of loneliness, paranoia, or depression
- Apathy or general lack of interest
- Change in personal priorities
  (Focus Adolescent Services, 2008)

Why do children and youth turn to alcohol abuse? Many may have a family history of substance abuse, and the cycle is created early. Dependence is already part of the genetic code. Often, youth are depressed and numb themselves with the alcohol. Many youths feel like they don't fit in or are out of the mainstream and are looking for acceptance. It has been proven over and over again that youths will experiment with alcohol as part of the growing up experience. Peer pressure and wanting to be included is also a key factor in the usage of alcohol.

Alcohol abuse can affect a youth's self-esteem and self-concept. It may give him or her an inflated sense of self or power. This inflated sense of self may lead to risky behaviors or allow them to become victims of physical and sexual abuse by stronger individuals.

Alcohol abuse also impacts coordination so youths with addiction issues are more prone to accidents and physical bodily harm. It also impacts their ability to make rational decisions and impairs their ability to engage in critical thinking. Their ability to problem solve is severely compromised and they often make the wrong decisions and create more chaos for themselves.

Family and peer relationships are also affected in that the alcohol abuser is often distant and uncommunicative and will become secretive about their actions and involvements. Family members become frustrated at not being able to reach the youth and know that they are losing him or her to alcohol and drug addiction.

How can alcohol abuse affect school performance and involvement? Fatigue may set in as the youth is often unable to get up to go to school, and if they do get up, they are often late. Discipline problems may arise because teachers call them on their lack of involvement or participation. Decline in grades occurs due to either lack of interest in school, lack of completing assignments, or failure to study for tests and quizzes.

A rise in absences may occur. Low self-esteem sets in because the youth is unsuccessful in school, and a sense of failure often sets in. This sense of failure may have a negative effect on peer relationships and parental relationships. Parents and school officials become concerned, and the youth now becomes the focus of attention—exactly the kind of attention that these youths want to avoid. This, in turn, may lead to running away or total withdrawal and becoming uncommunicative.

What can parents and schools do to help these individuals? Teach students to be involved in extracurricular activities, as research has shown that youths involved in sports activities and belonging to teams or organizations are less likely to abuse alcohol. Educate parents to the importance of connecting with their children and knowing where they are.

It is necessary to have a network of communication; in this way a parent knows where the youth is at all times. Cognitive Based Therapy (CBT) is a recognized and proven psychological strategy to deal effectively with alcohol abuse. By providing D.A.R.E. or similar programs early in schooling, youths are exposed to the dangers of alcohol and drug use and abuse.

Introduce and support substance-free parties, which have been growing in popularity when they have been monitored closely by adults. The right type of planning and organization has started to change attitudes regarding the use of alcohol at parties. Above all, it is important to talk with the child specifically about what thoughts or feelings may have caused their alcohol abuse and try to find a positive replacement.

What is Cognitive Behavioral Therapy (CBT)? It is a form of psychotherapy that is based on the theory that our cognitive thoughts affect our behaviors and feelings and not the people and things around us. The importance of this program is that we can change those thoughts to improve our behaviors and feelings (National Association of Cognitive Behavioral Therapists, 2009) A person who is taking part in cognitive therapy can learn to change harmful behavior patterns, such as alcohol abuse, by learning new skills to cope with these problems (about.com, 2010).

The goal of CBT is to work with the student to discuss what the direct thoughts are that are causing them to want to drink and work through strategies to cope with and eventually change those feelings. As a caring adult you must work with the student to help them feel comfortable with a person they can talk to if they are having thoughts or feelings that are causing them to drink, and reinforce the learned coping skills.

Teachers in schools can be aware of coping skills taught and help reinforce them especially when a youth is struggling within the classroom context. Teachers can also help the student to get involved in positive rewarding activities that can be used as replacements for drinking. School counselors and classroom teachers can help the youth get involved in alcohol-free social groups.

Many organizations such as Alcoholics Anonymous and their teen programs can get youths and their families help. Schools are active in promoting antidrug and alcohol abuse programs. Adults who work with this population must be aware that youth will be attracted to substance abuse if they do not have the skills to manage the chaos or challenges that are present in their lives.

We need to give children coping and problem-solving skills early on in their development. It cannot be assumed that they will just pick up these skills by watching the adults in their lives. Oftentimes the adults cannot be good or effective role models because of their own dysfunction. We need to teach skills to prevent alcohol abuse.

PRESCRIPTION FOR DANGER: PRESCRIPTION DRUG ADDICTION

In 2009 we started to hear more and more about a new phenomenon that was becoming prevalent in upper socioeconomic societies. Youth were engaging in risky and dangerous behaviors while under the influence of prescription drugs. These drugs were not being sold on the street but were being obtained right in in the family's medicine cabinet. Prescription drugs are the second-most commonly abused form of drug in America (second only to marijuana).

"A report out from the Centers for Disease Control and Prevention shows that despite an overall drop in illicit drug use, deaths from prescription drug use among people age 15 to 24 more than doubled between 1999 and 2005." "The numbers of new users of prescription drugs nonmedicinally in 2008 alone were 2.4 million for pain relievers, 1.2 million for tranquilizers, 793,000 for stimulants, and 240,000 for sedatives" (Office of National Drug Policy, 2009).

Why is this a problem? Because Prescription Drugs are readily available in almost every home, easily obtained, not perceived to be as serious as other illegal drugs or alcohol, potentially deadly to small children and youth even in small doses, and commonly not talked about with kids as a risk!

What is in the medicine cabinet? The most common types of prescription drugs includ: the stimulants Adderal, Ritalin, and Concerta; the depressants

Valium and Xanax; and the pain relievers OxyContin, Lorcet, Lortab, Percocet, Tylonol, and Vicodin.

One may ask if this is really abuse. It should be stressed that anytime a prescription drug is used for nonmedical purposes, it is considered abuse.

What to Look For: Changes in Personality

Change in appearance; child seems very vague, apathetic, disinterested, or out of it. Child is constantly complaining of illnesses or aches and requesting medication with no actual sign of illness or injury.

There are some very specific short-term effects: sleepiness or drowsiness, nausea, constipation, trouble concentrating, respiratory depression.

The long-term effects are

Addiction—uncontrolled, compulsive use of the drug.

Physical dependence—the body becomes used to having it in its system and depends on it to function.

Drug interactions—Occurs when taken together with substances such as alcohol or other types of drugs. These interactions can be fatal. Withdrawal is when the body becomes physically dependent on the drug; the body will go into a state of withdrawal if drug use is suddenly stopped or the amount is reduced significantly.

Withdrawal symptoms (e.g., nausea, depression, sleep disorders, diarrhea, sweating, anxiety, seizures, and respiratory failure) range in severity and can even be life-threatening. For this reason, withdrawal should be supervised by a medical professional to help reduce and control these effects as much as possible.

Respiratory depression—Can cause death if severe drug interactions occur. Impaired balance (depressants) where individual may fall and break bones. Impaired memory (depressants) where individual may black out and have no memory of behaviors or actions taken. Increase in body temperature (stimulants) where heart races and individual becomes very agitated or hyperactive. Irregular heartbeat (stimulants) where there is the possibility of stroke or heart attack.

What can parents do? Parents can hide all medications in a secure location, which may not be the bathroom medicine cabinet. Discard any prescription medications that are left over or expired. Alert grandparents who visit or host their grandchildren that their prescriptions should always be locked up and hidden away, including individual pills, which curious toddlers may put into their mouths. Monitor a teenager's Internet use for shopping on pharmaceutical Web sites. Discuss with neighbors and parents of your child's friends the importance of keeping prescription medications locked away.

What can be done? Educators can interact with and talk to kids! The best way to raise awareness about drugs is to talk about it. Schools districts have developed awareness and educational programs as part of this information-sharing campaign at the middle and high schools.

What can teachers do? Develop Awareness in the Classroom! Create posters with pictures of drugs and their characteristics so kids know what they're dealing with. Show children what can physically happen to their bodies as a result of different drug types. Brainstorm ways of dealing with stress and peer pressure so students have options. Develop a no-tolerance policy within your school and classroom. Discuss what fun things children can do instead of doing drugs. Celebrate Red-Ribbon Week and being drug-free. Teach children how to "Just Say No." Connect with parents and families about drug prevention outside of school.

This type of pathology is totally preventable with common sense, good security, and drug control. It is important to remember that this pathology develops because the individual is often looking to become numb, as they are unable to solve problems. The adults need to be aware of these difficulties and be ready to offer problem-solving skills that will give the youth a choice of options and strategies rather than taking the prescription drugs. It is a matter of timing.

Chapter 7

Violence and Weapons

What is the fascination that people have with weapons? Some collect them, some display them, and others use them as a form of destruction and power. Over and over we hear about some country making threats with nuclear weapons and bombs. The rest of the world responds in horror and with amazing speed to defuse the situation. Economic embargoes, rationing, protests, and marches all are used to prevent the individual country from posing a threat to the security of its people, its neighbors, and the planet. People become engaged and enraged. Actions occur, and often there is a resolution.

In America no such thing happens with juveniles and the use of violence. It is an ongoing problem that grows year after year. More and more young people are dying at the hands of other juveniles. Gang activity and organizations have flourished throughout the country. Increasingly, conflicts are resolved at the end of a gun or a knife.

Somewhere along the historical path guns became a way of life. Guns had previously been used in war, hunting, and by gangsters. In the late twentieth century guns and violence developed at an alarming rate. Guns were everywhere, and youths were involved in school shootings, bullying attacks, gang warfare, and crime.

The latest data from the U.S. Centers for Disease Control and Prevention show that "3,184 children and teens died from gunfire in the United States in 2006—a 6 percent increase from 2005. This means one young life lost every two hours and 45 minutes, almost nine every day, 61 every week. Of these deaths, 2,225 were homicides, 763 were suicides and 196 were due to an accident or undetermined circumstances. Boys accounted for 2,815 of the deaths; girls for 369 deaths. It is sad to note that more than five times as many children and teens, 17,451 in all, suffered non-fatal gun injuries" (Children Defense Fund, 2009).

It is astounding the number of children and teens in America killed by guns in 2006. These statistics would fill more than 127 public school classrooms of 25 students each. "More preschoolers (63) were killed by firearms than law enforcement officers (48) killed in the line of duty. Black males ages 15 to 19 are almost five times as likely as their White peers and more than twice as likely as their Hispanic peers to be killed by firearms" (Children Defense Fund, 2009).

The differences in ethnicity are very apparent in that between 1979 and 2006, the yearly number of firearm deaths of White children and teens decreased by about 40 percent, but deaths of Black children and teens increased by 55 percent (Children Defense Fund, 2009).

"Since 1979, gun violence has ended the lives of 107,603 children and teens in America. Sixty percent of them were White; 37 percent were Black. The number of Black children and teens killed by gunfire since 1979 (39,957) is more than 10 times the number of Black citizens of all ages lynched throughout American history (3,437)" (Children Defense Fund, 2009).

The United States remains one of the few industrialized countries that does have a series of requirements to own a gun; however, the enforcement of these procedures is very inconsistent, and one can buy a gun on the black market very easily. "There are more than 270 million privately owned fire-arms in our country which is the equivalent of nine firearms for every 10 men, women and children" (Children Defense Fund, 2009).

"The United States has the highest rates of firearm-related deaths among industrialized countries, including homicide, suicide and unintentional deaths; young people are often the victims. Gun violence accounts for over 3,000 deaths and over 15,000 injuries each year among children and adolescents. The rate of firearm-related homicides for U.S. children younger than 15 years of age is nearly 16 times greater than the rates in 25 other industrialized countries combined" (Academy of Child and Adolescent Psychiatry, 2008).

There are several reasons why kids are becoming more violent. This list was composed as a way to help individuals become much more aware of how children are becoming violent. The www.nssc1.org/physical-attacks-and-school-violence.html does an excellent job of describing all the warning signs for children or youth who may be prone to acting out physically or with weapons.

1. Home atmosphere—What happens in the home provides the role modeling for future behaviors. Parents that are violent create violent children.
2. Schools have begun to make students more accountable. Zero tolerance and making safety measures more stringent is leading to better protection.

3. Group effect—violent attitude can occur as a result of group effect. The company one keeps will influence the likelihood of acting out behaviors. If children are part of aggressive groups, they are more likely to act aggressively instead of assertively.
4. Easy availability of weapons—In America it is very easy to buy a gun on the black market or in some neighborhoods. Illegal guns have become instruments of the destruction of kids and their lives both as a victim and perpetrator.
5. Guards not checking properly—Many American schools have metal detectors, bag searches, and random locker searches; however, there is no consistency in many of the training of personnel who are inconsistent in their enforcement of the rules and do not do a good job of following procedures as guns and weapons make their way into the schools on a daily basis.
6. Depression and stress—Children and youth have an enormous amount of stress, anxiety, and depression in their daily lives. If you want them to become better problem solvers and cope with being a youth in the twenty-first century, you need to provide them with proper support (School violence and NCCS, 2010).

Violence at school often involves the use of weapons, which can be knives, guns, scissors, rulers, and any material that is often found within a tradition classroom. Traditionally, weapons prohibited on school grounds are firearms and explosives, but recently, many states have widened these guidelines to have weapons include firearms, explosive devices, bludgeons, metal knuckles, throwing stars, electronic stun guns, specific types of knives (such as switchblades and butterfly knives), and any weapon that "expels a projectile by the action of an explosive" (e.g., gunpowder).

Other states have gone much further than these specifications. Georgia defines weapons in its school laws as items complying with these descriptions: any pistol, revolver, or any weapon designed or intended to propel a missile of any kind, or any dirk, bowie knife, switchblade knife, ballistic knife, any other knife having a blade of three or more inches, straightedge razor, razor blade, spring stick, metal knuckles, blackjack, any bat, club, or other bludgeon-type weapon, or any flailing instrument consisting of two or more rigid parts connected in such a manner as to allow them to swing freely, which may be known as a nun chahka, nun chuck, nunchaku, shuriken, or fighting chain, or any disc, of whatever configuration, having at least two points or pointed blades which is designed to be thrown or propelled and which may be known as a throwing star or oriental dart, or any weapon of like kind, and any stun gun or taser.

The Web site www.nssc1.org/weapons-used-during-school-violence.html does an excellent job of describing the following weapons in that it clearly articulates what the weapons are and what their purposes are.

Handheld Items

1. Knife: One of the most common handheld items used by the school children of the rural and the suburban schools. Knives are easily accessed and will be used for threatening, assault, and even murder.
2. Hockey sticks: Available everywhere in a community and provide a solid instrument to wound or disable someone quickly.
3. Baseball bats: Also readily available inside the school compounds, especially in the playgrounds. Baseball, after all, is one of America's favorite pastimes. Where there are kids, there will be baseball bats available to inflict harm.

Arms—Weapons

1. Handgun: There are two major sources from which children can normally access a handgun. First, they can buy them on the street through gang connections. The second includes the negligence of parents who abandon their licensed firearms unintentionally and leave them unlocked or unsupervised where children and youth can easily take them and use them.
2. Machine pistol: It is actually a type of micro semi-machine gun. Machine pistols are usually confined to external gangs that indulge in serious crimes like burglary, extortion, intimidation, and so on. It is one of the most commonly used weapons during the "turf line" (territorial) wars and drive by shootings.
3. Assault rifles: Not commonly used in attacks in schools. These rifles are referred to as AK-47, AK-74, M4 Carbine, and are some of the most common examples of assault rifles. They are used frequently by the military in war zones. The Columbia High School Shooting incident which occurred in 1999 was a 13-year-old boy who fired an AK-47 at his school mates (School violence and NCSS, 2010).

The only instances in which all states allow weapons and firearms on school property are when individuals are authorized to do so; for example, when school police officers may be armed and teachers have instructional purposes. Many people wonder how many youth have access to weapons. "Recent data indicate that about 30 percent of young individuals own a firearm" (Brezina and Wright 2000). Further, a national study conducted by the Center for Disease Control revealed that in 2007 about one-fifth of high school students reported carrying a weapon to school.

In nearly all states, possession of a firearm on school property is a class C or class D felony. In addition to having the right to file criminal charges, all school districts have an automatic expulsion policy for students caught with any type of weapon on school property, although such action can be appealed on a case-by-case basis. Such policies are mandated by the Gun-Free Schools Act of 1994.

Special education students are protected from automatic expulsion under the Individuals with Disabilities Education Act (IDEA). A special education student who is found to possess a weapon on school grounds is subject to removal from the school to an interim setting for a period of up to forty-five days. During this time, the incident is studied, and if the possession of the weapon was not due to the student's disability that student can be punished in the same way as a non-special education student.

In nearly all states, parents can be held accountable for damages resulting from their child's criminal actions on school property, provided that child is living with the parents. This law means that parents of any student who vandalizes school property or attacks other students or teachers can be held liable. In addition, parents who allow minors access to firearms can be prosecuted on criminal charges, such as contributing to the delinquency of a minor.

Many states have adopted laws that require teachers to report a crime that they know or have reason to believe was committed on school property or at a school activity. Failure to do so may result in criminal prosecution for a misdemeanor. Lacking uniformity on this issue, school districts vary greatly with regard to making criminal charges (Everyday Law Encyclopedia 2010).

In reviewing weapon use and violent crime from 1993 to 2001, it was found that Blacks and Latinos were victims significantly disproportionate to their representation in the population. Blacks are twice as likely to be victims of weapon violence than Whites and half again as likely to be victims as Hispanics. Youths were also more likely to be victims of violent crime when a weapon is used than any other age group. Whites and Blacks age eighteen to twenty were more likely than Whites and Blacks of other ages to be victims of weapon violence, especially from guns.

The most vulnerable Hispanics to gun violence were those in the age groups of 15–17 and 18–20. Youths between the ages of 12 and 24 represented 40 percent of the U.S. population in 2001, but 44 percent of the gun crime victims and 46 percent of all weapon victims. Overall among victims, Hispanics were on average the youngest, followed by Blacks, then Whites. Youths between ages 18–20 were proportionately almost 3 times more likely to be a weapon victim than for a person of any other age group (BJS Special Report 2003).

Gun violence is a product of many issues in our society, including the erosion of the infrastructure necessary to support healthy child development. Some of these supports include adequate funding for comprehensive health-care, including coverage for mental illness and substance abuse, safe and appropriate housing, and effective education for all children.

Research associates the following risk factors with perpetration of youth violence (DHHS 2001; Lipsey and Derzon 1998; Resnick et al. 2004).

Individual Risk Factors

If a child has had the following experiences, he or she is more likely to have been exposed to or have a history of violent victimization and may have attention deficits such as hyperactivity or learning disorders. If there is a history of early aggressive behavior combined with involvement with drugs, alcohol, or tobacco, the youth is more likely to be involved in a series of violent acts.

Low IQ often results in making poor choices as the individual is unable to truly comprehend what is sometimes right and wrong. Youths with poor behavioral control often have not been taught how to self-regulate in productive ways. When there are deficits in social cognitive or information-processing abilities, the youth does not have the ability to use higher order thinking or critical thinking and problem-solving skills.

A youth who is under high emotional distress will make reactive choices that are often not in their best interests. Sometimes these choices cause even more havoc in their young lives. History of treatment for emotional problems, anti-social beliefs and attitudes, and exposure to violence and conflict in the family will also fuel the fire to an explosive response in a day-to-day situation.

Family Risk Factors

Some children and youth who grow up in certain types of families are more likely to use violence as a way to achieve their goals. It has been commonly known that authoritarian childrearing attitudes where there are very harsh punishments for actions will result in children living in fear and seeking out revenge.

Those children who are in lax or inconsistent disciplinary practices, low parental involvement and low emotional attachment to parents or caregivers will result in children who are unable to understand boundaries and expectations.

Low parental education and income often create very tense situations because of the financial needs and the lack of parenting skills. Many of these parents are in survival mode. Parental substance abuse or criminality does not provide good role models for children, and many become addicts or criminals themselves. This poor family functioning with very poor monitoring and supervision of children lends itself to kids not having any guidance or role models that show them what the right paths are.

Peer and Social Risk Factors

There are numerous studies that have shown that the association with delinquent peers, involvement in gangs, or social rejection by peers will often lead to a youth seeking other ways of belonging. Many youths have a lack of involvement in conventional activities, are aimless and roaming and often are bored, which lends itself to seeking out thrill activities that include a weapon.

These youths also have very poor academic performance and low commitment to school and school failure. They do not see the relevance or benefit of going to school. It is a place for losers, in their eyes. This type of thinking only continues the cycle of violence and poverty.

Community Risk Factors

If a youth lives in a diminished community where there are very few economic opportunities, high concentrations of poor residents, or high levels of transiency, there is more likelihood of violence. These youth do not see their lives getting any better and often will resort to crime as a way to get what they think they deserve. In these communities we often see very high levels of family disruption, low levels of community participation, or socially disorganized neighborhoods where everyone is too busy surviving to be anything else. The pride and safety of the community identity is not well-defined, and the residents do not want to be there; they are forced to live there because of their circumstances. This does not build investment into the community and the safety of its citizens.

Protective factors buffer young people from the risks of becoming violent. These factors exist at various levels. To date, protective factors have not been studied as extensively or as rigorously as risk factors. However, identifying and understanding protective factors are equally as important as researching risk factors.

Studies propose the following protective factors (DHHS 2001; Resnick et al. 2004):

Individual and Family Protective Factors

Intolerant attitude toward deviance
High IQ
High grade-point average

Positive social orientation
Religiosity
Connectedness to family or adults outside the family
Ability to discuss problems with parents
Perceived parental expectations about school performance are high
Frequent shared activities with parents
Consistent presence of parent during at least one of the following: when awakening, when arriving home from school, at evening mealtime or going to bed
Involvement in social activities
Peer and Social Protective Factors:
Commitment to school
Involvement in social activities

American children watch an average of three to four hours of television daily. By the age of eighteen, they will have witnessed over two hundred thousand incidents of violence. Television can be a powerful influence in developing value systems and shaping behavior. Unfortunately, much of today's television programming is violent.

Hundreds of studies of the effects of TV violence on children and teenagers have found that children may become "immune" or numb to the horror of violence, gradually accept violence as a way to solve problems, imitate the violence they observe on television, and identify with certain characters, victims, or victimizers. Today's television is more violent and explicit than the television of twenty or thirty years ago. At any time, a child can turn on the television and witness violence, explicit language, and scenes that are sometimes far more than suggestive. These shows are seen on cable, regular television, news, and cartoons.

Extensive viewing of television violence by children causes greater aggressiveness. Sometimes, watching a single violent program can increase aggressiveness. Children who view shows in which violence is very realistic, frequently repeated, or unpunished are more likely to imitate what they see. Children with emotional, behavioral, learning, or impulse control problems may be more easily influenced by TV violence. The impact of TV violence may be immediately evident in the child's behavior or may surface years later. Young people can even be affected when the family atmosphere shows no tendency toward violence.

Studies have shown that too much television may cause children to become immune or numb to the horror of violence. After seeing characters kill and hurt, children may not be able to differentiate the real-life violence of murder versus the onscreen make-believe violence. Children may also interpret that violence is a way to solve problems, imitating what they see on shows. Children on the playground are quick to make believe they are their favorite superhero fighting the bad guys. Too often children get hurt or hurt others, not realizing the severe consequences of what they see on television.

While TV violence is not the only cause of aggressive or violent behavior, it is clearly a significant factor. Parents can protect children from excessive TV violence in the following ways:

1. Pay attention to the programs their children are watching and watch some with them; set limits on the amount of time they spend with the television; consider removing the TV set from the child's bedroom
2. Point out that although the actor has not actually been hurt or killed, such violence in real life results in pain or death
3. Refuse to let the children see shows known to be violent, and change the channel or turn off the TV set when offensive material comes on, with an explanation of what is wrong with the program
4. Disapprove of the violent episodes in front of the children, stressing the belief that such behavior is not the best way to resolve a problem
5. To offset peer pressure among friends and classmates, contact other parents and agree to enforce similar rules about the length of time and type of program the children may watch (AACAP, 2010)

Do all the violent acts that children view on television cause them to commit crimes in their later lives? Research has been vigilant in trying to answer this question. First, not all violent acts have the same impact. Some acts that are witnessed have a tendency to repel and disgust children, so they are less likely to imitate those specific acts. It is the acts that create a curiosity that are more likely to be repeated or attempted. The desires to have the same results as seen on television are what propel the youth to want to try the activity.

Are the effects of watching TV violence brief or lasting? The answer depends on the child's or youth's ability to tell the difference between what is real and what is imaginary. If a child has severe emotional distress, mental health, or adjustment issues, they are more likely to emulate or idealize what they see on television. They will have difficulty being able to differentiate and therefore are more likely to act out.

Is TV as important a factor in fostering societal violence as economic poverty, bad schools, and broken homes? One can argue that many things influence children while they are developing into adults. The societal factors definitely define their points of reference. How much weight can we attribute to television violence is still a work in progress.

If a child lives in a dangerous community, goes to an unsafe school, lives in an abusive family, and watches violent shows on television, how can we figure out which of these factors has the most influence in the youth becoming violent? A child demonstrates what he or she is familiar with and has been proven to get the child what he or she wants. We cannot blame television as the sole condition responsible for child and youth violence. Does this play a role? Absolutely! However one must be careful not to oversimplify this correlation.

Nobody is born violent. A child becomes violent because of the kind of environment that has been provided to him or her. Parents, teachers, and schools together can create a child with the right attitude, but it can only be done by providing the right kind of environment and care to the child. If a child is under severe depression or under any kind of stress and anxiety, then he or she can suffer from the problem of violent attitude.

Violent attitude includes everything like bullying, threatening, beating, theft, larceny, and vandalism, and so on. Kids who are having high amounts of violent attitude can kill other people as well, like Dylan Klebold and Eric Harris killed one teacher and twelve students in the Columbine High School massacre incident that took place in the 1999. An additional twenty-one people were injured in this incident.

Other incidents like the Bath School Disaster, Virginia Tech massacre, and University of Texas massacre are other examples of dreadful school violence. All of these incidents involved weapons of one sort or another. The key to understanding the violence is the availability of the weapons, the thinking and planning that occurs prior to the attacks, and the results of the use of weapons.

There have been countless reports of gang development and activity in schools and in communities. The key is to know what to look for in terms of factors. There are three levels of gang activity that you should be aware of. Those levels include hardcore "wannabes" that emulate gang activity and business people who provide gang-related services to students engaging in gang activity or who may potentially engage in gang activity. The first two may exist on school grounds, while the others sneak their way into the path of gang members or potential gang members.

Gangs have been shown to be one of the leading factors in the growth of violent crimes in recent years, both on and off school property. To become a gang member, an initiation usually needs to be passed. This often consists of violent acts like fighting, drive-by shootings, gang rape, and murder. Gang involvement puts a child at risk of getting arrested, getting badly hurt, or even getting killed.

Gang involvement almost always includes alcohol and drug use. A child's involvement in a gang puts their entire family at risk for retaliation from other gangs that they have messed with. Many members of youth gangs go on to be adult offenders who spend much of their lives in and out of prison, if they live that long. Most gang members end up dropping out of school or being expelled. If a child is in a gang, then he or she is likely around and even handling guns and other weapons.

Identifying gang members is often tricky and requires increased awareness of the subtleties that are present. There are also observable indicators that can tell you if there are gang members within your school. Those indicators are

1. The wannabes tend to wear hats, scarves, and jackets that resemble one another. They may also all have the same haircut. Hardcore gang members tend to refrain from this behavior, making them more difficult to spot.
2. They may all wear the same colors.
3. Their shoelaces may all be the same. Sometimes gang members are more subtle in their uniformity, so it is important to look at every detail.
4. They may wear a uniform pendant on their jackets.
5. There may be graffiti on their notebooks and on other items that belong to them. Symbols to look for include the Star of David, pitchfork, six points, and six dots (School Violence NCSS, 2010).

Gangs have access to weapons because they are often able to move through communities and schools undetected. The power of the group allows them to engage in drug selling, prostitution, intimidation, and extortion. The money they accumulate allows them to buy the latest weapons. These weapons become their security and protection from other violent gangs and the police. The majority of the crimes involving gang members are gun related.

Gangs that are unaddressed within schools can become excessively violent. They can recruit new individuals and engage in initiation activities that can be harmful, bring weapons to school, get into gang fights on school property during school hours and put other students at risk, sell drugs and do drugs, and ultimately resort to violence if they do not get their way with another student.

Becoming a gang member has a price. The price is not cheap. Gangs are a specialized part of society and a very exclusive club. Gang members and investigators have reported the following acts as a part of gang initiation: fighting another gang member, usually until the last man is standing; killing an animal, oftentimes someone's beloved pet; theft ranging from petty theft to car theft and even muggings with a weapon; drive-by shootings; gang rape; and murder .For female gang members, degrading sexual acts with groups of men and women (School Violence, NCCS, 2010).

The youths who want to join a gang will do so to get a feeling of power, control, or to belong. What many of them do not understand when first getting involved is that they will most likely be required to use a weapon in their school or community. They often do not realize the ramifications of using a weapon till it is too late and there is someone dead or wounded in front of them.

Many youths do not have the mental maturity to process the result of their actions. They have committed a crime that is life changing. Weapons and violence have now captured another young life and denied this country an important resource. Another statistic! Another prison inmate! Another fatality!

SOLUTIONS AND INTERVENTIONS

School uniforms have been identified as a possible solution to gang violence and violence in general in schools. Educators thought that this might be the magic pill solution. Unfortunately, years later the research has shown that there was a decrease in school disciplinary issues but not violence. Uniforms do help in identification of students from a specific school but the key is to manage the violence in the community, as that seems to have much more of an impact on students acting out at school.

Mental services are paramount in the prevention of acting out behaviors. Studies have been conducted that show that the overall mental health and performance of students who have mental health services at their disposal, in the school, are able to cope with issues better. They feel that they have somewhere to go to acquire the help that they need. And if they are reluctant to seek help on their own, the school's mental health services allow both parents and teachers to arrange for counseling for students. All in all, mental health services within the school can lead to the prevention of school violence, thus resulting in the prevention of injuries and deaths that may occur. It has also been found that school-based mental health services are one of the most cost-effective ways of preventing violence within schools.

Community involvement and participation is one key to changing the tide of youth violence. In a community where resources like community centers and after-school programs are available, children are given alternatives to finding trouble to get into after school. School curriculum that enforces the rules for all students, not just some, supports the community's role in helping to decrease school violence for children of all ages.

Remember that a community is composed of individuals who share common goals, interests and living areas, not just houses, stores, schools, and churches. When people come together as a community collaborative, with the objective of helping to decrease school violence, the safety in numbers is evident.

Schools and school districts have a responsibility to manage and end school violence. To prevent violence, school districts have responded in different ways. These ways include alternative programs, expulsion, suspension, locker searches, metal detectors, mentoring programs, closed lunches, dress codes, support groups, security guards, and conflict mediation training for teachers and administrators. The solution simply depends on the type of violence facing the school district and its severity. Unfortunately, budgets usually dictate the degree of safety children receive.

Students can contribute in a very important manner in preventing school violence. Hence, they need to be involved strongly in the fight against school violence. Students must go through workshops that focus on anger management skills and positive attitude. They must be taught right from the start to focus on the positive aspects of any person or thing rather than just despise the negative aspects. This attitude will help them in dealing with all kinds of people and situations in life. Teachers as well as parents play an important role in developing a child's attitude toward life.

Students should be inculcated with values of friendship and care by their teachers in school. When a student finds any of his peers in a low or depressive mood, acting in an aggressive or violent manner, getting into use of drugs, bullying other students or being bullied by others, carrying dangerous weapons or talking about creating any kind of menace in class or school, the student should take immediate action by bringing the matter in front of the higher school authorities. The school authorities can then take all adequate measures to stop any form of violence that could come up and get in touch with the parents of the student indulging in any of the above activities and work toward counseling them out of their negative.

There are many things that can be done to prevent school violence and use of weapons in the schools. The National School Safety Council promotes these 10 things as excellent possible strategies: If you want to save children from school violence then ten things can be done-

1. Close watch: Children need supervision, attention, and ongoing monitoring. Parents who know where their children are and what they are involved in usually have a much higher success at teaching kids to make the right choice.
2. Appointment of counselors: Schools need to give kids access to counselors. These counselors are often on the front line helping kids deal with issues that arise on a daily basis. Their specialized knowledge in psychology, family systems, and mental health give them the background and expertise to deal effectively with troubled youth.
3. Friendly relationship: Parents are the child's first teacher. The child is connected to the parent and will observe the actions of the adults. Healthy and good role modeling on the part of the parents goes a long way to building trusting and safe relationships.

4. Support from teachers: Teachers are in the forefront regarding school violence. Teachers can inform and teach about the negative effect of having violent attitudes and how this negative attitude can ruin their future. Professional development, training, and guidance needs to be given to teachers on an ongoing basis to give them the skills needed to guide students in having more positive attitudes and better problem-solving skills.

5. Love and care: Love and affection are the best medicine to cure violent attitudes among children. Children who feel love and respect do not hurt others. Parents and teachers need to teach children about respect and tolerance for all.

6. Weapons: Illegal access to weapons needs to end immediately if we are going to prevent children from using weapons in schools. Children can buy weapons easily right in their own neighborhoods. History is full of such cases where children had used weapons in schools and killed children and teachers.

7. Fame: Students want fame and recognition. Using violence to become infamous is a twisted way of looking at attention. We need to get kids to be recognized in non-violent ways.

8. Encourage other habits: It is the duty of parents and teachers to encourage positive interests and habits. Busy kids do not go out and shoot others. Schools need to offer many types of after-school activities and keep youths off the streets between 3–7 pm.

9. Praise: Parents and teachers need to praise children for their good deeds and actions. Children need to be recognized, rewarded, and reinforced for making good choices and doing the right thing. It does not matter if it is intrinsic or extrinsic rewards or recognition; it just needs to happen.

10. Friends: Friends are a major influence in decreasing violent attitude. Friends can provide full guidance and cooperation to the students who are more likely to act out violently. These friends can help them in solving their problems. It is a known fact that if you teach violent youths to solve their problems in a creative and positive way the results will often be a reduction in violent attitude (School Violence, NSSC 2010).

The following recommendations have been given for parents as a way to halt violence permanently. These recommendations are quite similar to what is presented above. It is only in collaboration that we can put an end to this problem.

The following are the ten things that parents can do to prevent violence:

1. Continuous supervision: Quality time with children equals better understanding of their children and better monitoring of their notorious activities.
2. Get some counseling help: School and family counseling do lead to family changes in dealing with conflict, behavior, and acting out. It is a support that is often available but not used consistently.
3. Develop friendship: Parents need to develop communication, trust, respect, and responsibility with their children. Developing relationships that include friendship will result in a child seeking guidance or help prior to making a decision.
4. Teachers' help and guidance: Teachers are the second closest to children after their parents, as they spend half of their day in school. Teachers can be the sounding board and help develop positive attitudes to solving conflict. They can model appropriate responses and help children learn how to make better choices.
5. Give love and warmth: Love is the way to build children's sense of belonging and value. A child who feels valued and appreciated will be more likely to be caring and nurturing than violent. We need to create caring and responsive children.
6. Access to arms: Guns and pistols are available easily and can be accessed by children easily. The answer is stricter gun control in all communities. No access means less crime.
7. Popularity: Children who use violence as a way to get popularity are often very lonely individuals who are seeking some level of attention so that people will know they exist. Children need to learn how to ask for what they need and not have violence as the instrument to get their needs and demands met.
8. Inculcate other interests: Children should be exposed to a variety of different activities in order to take their minds off of more violent activities. A bored child seeks trouble; a busy one is too occupied having fun and learning. The solution to preventing children and youth from partaking in violence is to build their interests and to give them the time to explore as many new options as possible.
9. Compliment: Parents and teachers should compliment children frequently. Catch them being good and let them know that you as the adult appreciate them and their actions.
10. Relationships: Peers and positive adult relationships go a long way in shaping and directing child and youth behavior. The key is to make sure

that they have access to the right people, right friends, and right experiences and activities (School Violence, NSSC 2010).

Following these ten steps can make the child's life violence free, and they would be able to concentrate more on their future.

In conclusion, violence and weapons go hand in hand. They work together as a united partnership. Violence will continue as long as weapons are available to youth and children. Teaching children about the consequences of weapon violence needs to begin early. Children need to understand and respect weapons. They have to be taught from an early age what is the role of a weapon. They have to be denied access to weapons, and parents need to become vigilant in their control of guns. Children and youth need to be taught consistent conflict mediation and problem-solving skills.

Communication and awareness are the secrets to successfully managing this epidemic we are facing in America. Parents, teachers, politicians, children, youth, and community agencies all have to become onboard in fighting the daily battle of violence. This awareness and collective participation is what will begin to make a difference. Saying no to guns and violence and saying yes to peace and kindness can begin the journey of living in harmony.

If there is no change in the near future, America will become a wasteland of shattered dreams and wasted lives. A country where its youth die at the hands of their peers. America will be a place where no one is safe to pursue the dream of living a complete and safe life in their community.

The American dream will no longer be to pursue happiness and the good life, but rather to survive in a hostile environment and to live another day.

Chapter 8

Life on the Street

Homelessness and Street Children

> The worst sin towards our fellow creatures is not to hate them, but to be indifferent to them; that is the essence of inhumanity.
>
> —From *The Devil's Disciple* by George Bernard Shaw

Street children is a term used to refer to children who live on the streets of a city. They are basically deprived of family care and protection. Most children on the streets are between the ages of five and seventeen years old, and their population between different cities is varied. Street children live in junk boxes, parks, or on the street itself. A great deal has been written defining street children, but the primary difficulty is that there are no precise categories, but rather a continuum, ranging from children who spend some time in the streets and sleep in a house with ill-prepared adults, to those who live entirely in the streets and have no adult supervision or care.

A widely accepted set of definitions commonly attributed to Amnesty International divides street children into two main categories:

1. Children *on* the street are those engaged in some kind of economic activity ranging from begging to vending. Most go home at the end of the day and contribute their earnings to their family. They may be attending school and retain a sense of belonging to a family. Because of the economic fragility of the family, these children may eventually opt for a permanent life on the streets.
2. Children *of* the street actually live on the street (or outside of a normal family environment). Family ties may exist but are tenuous and are maintained only casually or occasionally (Wikipedia 2010).

Street children exist in many major cities, especially in developing countries, and may be subject to abuse, neglect, exploitation, or even, in extreme cases, murder by "cleanup squads" hired by local businesses or police. In Latin America a common cause is abandonment by poor families unable to feed all their children. In Africa, an increasingly common cause is the killing of parents by AIDS or rendering them unable to care for their children.

The United Nations has been attributed as estimating the population of street children worldwide at 150 million, with the number rising daily. These young people are more appropriately known as community children, as they are the offspring of our communal world. "Ranging in age from three to eighteen, about 40 percent of those are homeless—as a percentage of world population, unprecedented in the history of civilization. The other 60 percent work on the streets to support their families. They are unable to attend school and are considered to live in "especially difficult circumstances." Increasingly, these children are the defenseless victims of brutal violence, sexual exploitation, abject neglect, chemical addiction, and human rights violations.

That means nearly 1 of every 60 people living on the planet is a child living on the streets. Half of them die within the first four years of their street life. In other words, a child who ends up in the street at age 8 has a 50 percent chance of dying before the age of 12. Reasons for becoming street children include extreme poverty of a family, death of parents, unstable socio-economic situation in the country, and armed conflicts that cause many people to flee their homes, therefore instigating many families to fall apart.

"Once on the street, children must resort to begging, robbery, and even prostitution in order to survive. Many join gangs where they are introduced to crime, violence, and drugs. They become addicted to inhaling glue, paint thinner, and/or other toxic substances destroying brain cells and organ tissues" (P.Shukla,2010).

Neglected by society and government, street children are deprived of education, proper nutrition, and medical care. They suffer and die from various, often easily treatable, diseases such as head lice, skin parasites, pneumonia, tuberculosis, and a host of sexually transmitted diseases, including, yet not limited to, gonorrhea, syphilis, and AIDS. Because of the grave lack of outreach and shelter programs, street children often have no place to go and no one from whom they can seek help and protection.

In defining street children, UNICEF classifies them in two categories: street working and street living. Most children that are commonly referred to as "street children" in the developing world actually live at home but spend much of the day working in the streets.

Many believe the most serious threat to street children comes from the very people responsible for their safety and protection—local governmental and law enforcement officials. Unfortunately, police brutality and corruption is common worldwide, and is especially widespread in developing countries with large populations of street children. "Unspeakable police brutality reflects the governments' perception of street children as parasites to be exterminated, rather than as children needing homes and nurturing" (Eugenia Berezina, 2003).

Street children are found throughout the world. Below you will find a summary of the latest statistics: Street children may be found on every inhabited continent in a large majority of the world's cities. The following estimates indicate the global extent of street child populations.

- India 11 million
- Egypt 1.5 million
- Pakistan 1.5 million
- U.S. 750,000—1 million
- Kenya 250,000—300,000
- Philippines 250,000
- Congo 250,000
- Morocco 30,000
- Brazil 25,000
- Germany 20,000
- Honduras 20,000
- Jamaica 6,500
- Uruguay 3,000
- Switzerland 1,000
  (Wikipedia, 2010)

Street Children in the Developing World

The following statistics were collected by the Consortium for Street Children and highlight the urgency for action, as the need is so overwhelming.

- In Cambodia, 9,642 children live in extreme poverty in Sihanoukville's streets and slums, and are denied their basic rights.1,876 children (958 girls) under 14 years work on the streets and beaches (Dept. of Social Affairs, 2007).
- There are an estimated 400,000 street children and child laborers in Lima (Peru) alone (Christian Solidarity International).
- Out of an estimated 8,000 Street Children in Uganda around 4,000 children live on the streets of Kampala, the Ugandan capital. Many are war or AIDS orphans and some are HIV positive (Jubilee Action).
- Brazil has the third-largest amount of working children in Latin America. According to the ILO, 7,860 children and adolescents in eight cities in Rio are working in painful and unhealthy conditions (ILO/Jubilee Action).

- In Addis Ababa, over 30 percent of girls aged 10–14 do not live with their parents; of the 30 percent, 20 percent have run away from child marriages (UNICEF).
- Worldwide, 77 million children do not attend school. In Ethiopia, 5 million children are not in school (UNICEF).
- In 2006, there were 700,000 girls working in homes in Delhi alone (Save the Children).
- There are over 50,000 street children in Nairobi with estimates of 10 percent growth per year (Global March).
- There are more than 50 million street children in Latin America alone (Casa Alianza).
- At least 1 million street children live in Russia. Most of these children are "social orphans," meaning they have at least one living parent (Child Aid to Russia and the Republics).
- The commercial sex trade in Kenya involves about 10,000 to 30,000 children (Child Hope).
- 95 percent of girls living on the streets of Ethiopia experience sexually exploitation (Child Hope).
- An estimated 10 to 15,000 children are abandoned by their parents in Akwa Ibom and Cross River states in Nigeria due to the belief that they are witches (Stepping Stones Nigeria),
- UNICEF's estimate of 11 million street children in India is considered to be conservative. The Indian Embassy estimates that 314,700 street children live in metros such as Bombay, Calcutta, Madras, Kanpur, Bangalore, and Hyderabad and 100,000 in Delhi alone (Railway Children).
- Around 1 million children are believed to be in Egypt's streets, mostly in Cairo and Alexandria (Consortium for Street Children).
- Of an estimated 400,000 street children in Bangladesh, nearly 10% resort to prostitution for survival (Consortium for Street Children).
- 88 percent of street children in Phnom Penh, Cambodia, have had sexual relations with tourists (VIVA).
- There are 600 ragpicker children working in dump yards in Rafiquagar (Mumbai) and Sathenagar (Kalyan) (Hindustani Covenant Church/ Hope for children).
- In Morogoro, Tanzania, AIDS and poverty were the push factors for 400 orphans to live on the street (International Children's Trust).
- 6000 children live on the street in Durban, South Africa (Umthombo/Amos trust).
- There are an estimated 40 million street children and street working children in Latin America (UNICEF).

- In 2006, there were 21,140 street children and 7,170 street mothers under 20 in Accra (Street Child Africa).
- In San Juan de Lurigancho and Cercado de Lima, there are 5000 working children, 300 street children in both towns, and 25,000 children at risk of taking to the street (Red Viva/Toybox).
- Between 4 and 5 adolescents are murdered daily and every 12 minutes a child is beaten. (Brazil's National Movement of Street Children)
- More than 600 children sleep on the streets of Kharkiv, Ukraine and some of the teenagers have been there over 7 years. 300,000 children are outside the school system in Ukraine and are not accounted for. 97% of children that leave orphanages become homeless (Depaul Foundation).
- An estimated 100–150 million children live and/or work on the streets across the world (EveryChild).
- 82 percent of the street children in Cairo & Alexandria go to the streets due to child abuse at home or work (UNODC).
- In St. Petersburg, between 2004 and 2005, 70 percent of the street children tested HIV Positive (Consortium on Street Children).
- An estimated 60–90 percent of street children in Mumbai are sexually active (Indianngos).
- Up to 90 percent of street children use psychoactive substances, including medicines, alcohol, cigarettes, heroin, cannabis, and industrial products such as shoe glue. (Casa Alianza).
- In a 1991 study of 143 Guatemalan street children, one hundred percent of the children had been sexually abused (Global Impact).
- The average age of a street child in South Africa is 13 (Johann Le Roux (1996).
- Nearly 60 percent of street children in Kenya report police brutality (IRIN).
- An estimated 90 percent of street children in Bucharest are raped on their first night (BBCSource: Fact Sheet- Consortium on Street Children 2010).

As one looks over these statistics one can become totally discouraged by the statistics and the ugliness of life in this world. These fact sheets that are produced are a way to help all individuals become sensitized to the fact that we have issues in that we are not meeting the needs of many of our world children. Many countries do not have the resources to manage children and give them a quality of life that should be a human right.

Street Children in the Western World

There is a misconception that the Western world does not have a problem with missing children or homelessness or children being abused or taken advantage of the sex trade or child labor. In countries with very high standards of living every child should be provided for and taken care of in a respectful way. The following statistics indicate otherwise. The Western world is not immune to these horrific problems.

- In the past 5 years, up to 300 children go missing from state care in Ireland and an unknown number of these are feared to have been sex trafficked (Barnardos, Children and homelessness fact sheet, February 2008).
- Ireland has 500 to 1,000 street children (Council of Europe).
- 100,000 children run away from home in the UK each year with a quarter sleeping on the streets (World Street Children News).
- 1 in 7 children who run away in the UK experience violence and/or sexual assault while away (Still Running: Children on the Streets in the UK, 1999).
- 80 percent of UK runaways said they were running from problems at home (Still Running: Children on the Streets in the UK, 1999).
- Neither in Spain nor the rest of Europe does there exist reliable data about the number of children living in the streets (Canal Solidario, May 24 2004).
- The number of Moroccan minors entering Spain has risen steadily from 811 in 1998 to 3,500 in 2002 (CS Monitor).
  (Fact Sheet- Consortium on Street Children 2010).
- In Germany up to 20,000 runaway children, teenagers, and young adults live on the street at some time. (Terres des Hommes, Tuesday 8th September 2008).
- Every year in Germany, an estimated 9,000 young people run away from home: 70 percent are boys, 30 percent girls (Spiegel Online, Aug. 14, 2008).
- Only half of Roma and Sinti children in Germany attend school at all and of those who do attend, a high number (estimated 80 percent) attend "special schools" (EUMAP 2003).
- The number of youth living on the street in Prague is increasing and February 2006 estimates give a figure of 1,500 street children in Prague. The majority of these children in Prague come from children's homes (70 percent), the remaining part from broken families (Research Institute for Labour and Social Affairs, Prague 2006).
- 1 in 12 young runaways are hurt or harmed while they are away (Children's Society).
- 1 in 6 young runaways sleep rough (Children's Society).
- There are only 11 safe refuge beds for runaway children in the whole of the UK (Railway Children).

- 100,000 children under the age of 16 run away from home or care every year in the UK (Children's Society).
(Fact Sheet-Consortium on Street Children 2010).

The statistics listed above do show an increase in street children worldwide. It is sad to see that many are in a position of survival and that the prognosis is poor. The facts tell an impersonal story.

PERSONAL STORIES: These stories were collected from a variety of websites and this author did not interview them individually. The purpose of including these stories was to give the reader a firsthand account of what life is like on the streets in a variety of places throughout the world.

This story is from www.informationclearinghouse.info/article3573.htm. This story was written by Duncan Campbell in 2003. The unfortunate fact is that this issue is alive and well in 2011. Nothing much has changed in the quality of life for many of these children. The cycle continues. Duncan Campbell writes:

"Selvyn says he is 14 but he looks about eight. His feet are bare, his clothes torn and his eyes heavy with the effects of sniffing a powerful glue. His home is nearby, beneath the stars and beside a municipal rubbish dump. His neighbors are other street children—equally feral and ragged and loaded—and the hovering vultures which compete with them for scraps of food on the dump." Street children worldwide seem to follow a consistent pattern of survival, where they are almost invisible to some and very apparent to others as they harass the local citizens with their begging and stealing. Many of these street urchins are nothing more than a nuisance and an eyesore to many South American cities and culture.

There have been reports in the media that the killing of street children in Central America is out of control. There is no rhyme or reason to the killings. There is also no sure way of being able to predict and report accurate statistics on the amount of children exterminated or sold for organ harvesting.

In cities like Guatemala it is routine to see children dead on the side of the road. Their bodies defaced and showing evidence of having been tortured. There is recklessness in the attitude about these children. It is almost as if they are trash and are not fit for life. Human rights groups and Western governments agree that there is an epidemic of violence.

Campbell, in his exposé of this human tragedy, offers a few more personal examples of young people who survive on the streets. "Juan, 16, also lives beside the rubbish dump. It is a dangerous life, he says, because they can be attacked at any time by the police. 'Why do they attack us? Because they like to. Yes, it's dangerous but this is where we live.' At times the police are the worst offenders followed by rival gangs and people who just think it is amusing to attack and kill these street children.

A young man named Hector who was interviewed for the exposé written by Campbell said, "Everyone knows someone who has been killed," pointing to a place where he said the latest body had been found. Of the murder victims in February, the youngest was eight; there was also a 13-year-old, three 15-year-olds and four aged 16." The commonness of seeing young individuals killed and the laissez-faire attitude is astounding. One has become so used to the idea of dead children that it does not face these street youths. How completely wrong is that in our society in the twenty-first century?

Campbell goes on to report that not all on the streets are young men. "Maria, 17, carrying a baby even grubbier than herself, giggled as she talked about life on the street. Like many of the girls, she makes her money as a prostitute and spends it mainly on the powerful glue, Resistol, or marijuana." There seems to be very little option for young girls on the streets. It is either prostitute your body, or be attacked or killed.

There have been several attempts by a variety of South American governments to stop the killing and the ongoing genocide. Countries like Brazil still see an enormous amount of street children being killed or just disappearing without a trace. Agencies that are responsible for the reporting of the deaths are often not reliable, or the data that they are given or collect is skewed in some form to underrepresent the numbers.

Some of the major players in the attacks of street children are the police themselves. Many of them are hired as vigilante in their off-hours to do the cleansing. Several politicians in several countries (Honduras, Brazil, Guatemala) have indicated that the police officers doing these crimes will be brought to justice, although very few are ever seen within a judicial system. There is too much money to be made. Campbell reports that: "On the outskirts of the capital, in Comayaguela, Honduras lies the municipal cemetery and at its highest point is a place where the street children are buried. It is like looking at a small war cemetery, but the combatants are even younger: 13 and 14 and 15 and a few who have made it into their early 20s." "This tomb guards your body, God your soul and us your memory," says the message on one of the graves." One can just imagine the sadness in a place which is usually reserved for people who have lived a full life is populated by young people who should be in the prime of their lives.

As this story expresses there is a need to have an action plan for protection of children throughout the world. Knowing that there are many victims every day that continue to die and struggle is a violation of basic human rights. Our world needs to move forward and protect the children no matter what part of the world they are in.

Homelessness in the USA

It's estimated that more than 1.5 million U.S. youth run away or are sent away from home yearly; 68% are between the ages of 15–17 and 35% had run away before. Every year approximately 5,000 runaways and homeless youth die from assault, illness, and suicide. The number of runaways contacting federal outreach programs rose from 550,000 to 761,000 between 2002 and 2008. Behind the statistics lie stories waiting to be told of lives changed by the runaway experience (http://www2.lv.psu.edu/jkl1/runawaylives).

"For the 1,682,900 unaccompanied boys and girls most of them between the ages of 15 and 17 living on the street, homelessness is an even bigger challenge than it is for homeless adults. For kids, just by being homeless and on their own, they are breaking the law in many states. So often kids try to stay underground by avoiding shelters and other services that could help them get their lives together" (www.zimbio.com). The sad part is that many are very successful at avoiding the authorities and become statistics either as victims, or they end up dead.

Trying to define street youth is like trying to say that all the peas in a pod arc the same. There have been many attempts to define this population. The following definition as defined by the Street Connect Organization comes the closest, in my opinion. They define street youth as a "Youth population that is diverse, complex and heterogeneous. The generic term 'street youth'is made up of a number of subcultures including hard-core street entrenched young people, squatters, group home kids, child welfare kids, soft-core 'twinkies,' 'in-and-outers,' punks, runaways, throwaways, refugees and immigrants, young single mothers, and those who are homeless because their entire family are homeless" (www.streetconnect.org).

Within these makeshift "categories" are numerous descriptors that tend to signal street activities such as gang bangers, prostitutes, drug dealers, drug users, panhandlers, and squeegeeers. While there is considerable diversity in the age ranges considered by researchers, providers, and policy makers to define street youth, sixteen to twenty-four years of age is accepted by many as reflects both the age limits of many services and the age range of the social networks of many youths.

"Street youths are generally understood to be young people who do not have a permanent place to call home, and who instead, spend significant amount of time/energy on the street (e.g., in alleyways, parks, storefronts, dumpsters, etc.); in squats (located usually in abandoned buildings); at youth shelters and centers; and/or with friends (typically referred to as 'couch surfers')" (www.streetconnect.org).

"One study said that only about half of homeless teenagers make use of shelters, drop-in centers, etc. The other half, afraid of being sent home, put in foster care, or even put in jail, prefer to try to make it on their own. Many of them run away from home. But generally, kids don't run away just for fun, or adventure and those that do are likely to return home in a few days, instead of trying their luck at living out on the streets for the long term" (www.zimbio.com).

Many kids who run away are escaping from homes where they were physically, sexually, or emotionally abused. Others run from homes where their parents had serious substance abuse problems or mental illnesses. Some kids who run away are kids in foster care, who have grown tired of life in the foster care system and have decided they'd be better off on their own. Other kids are actually "throw-aways," kids who were thrown out or locked out of their families' homes. There are many reasons why this must happen. Kids get kicked out of their homes for reasons ranging from their own behavior problems, to girls admitting that they're pregnant, to teens whose parents find out they are gay, lesbian or bisexual.

There are kids who start out homeless because their families become homeless, but then become separated from their families. For instance, in many shelters for female victims of domestic violence, the shelters will not accept boys over a certain age. So a boy whose mother goes into a domestic violence shelter, perhaps taking the boy's younger siblings, may have to try and find his own place to stay (www.zimbio.com—Street Teenagers on their Own in America).

"There are some homeless teens who manage to continue going to school, but this is often very hard. For one thing, if a kid is in the position of having to hide from authority figures in order to avoid being returned to an abusive home or put in foster care, going to school would be out of the question because they'd probably be caught. If they do manage to go to school, it can be nearly impossible for a kid to keep up with homework and studies, when he is worrying about when he will eat again or where he will sleep tonight! So, for homeless teens, school often falls by the wayside" (zimbio.com 2010). There is no way to get an education if you are unable to get the basics in life such as food and shelter.

Plus, it can be nearly impossible for homeless teens to get legitimate employment that will give them a standard of living that is above the poverty line. Many homeless teens are under the legal working age, several of them can be as young as 12–14, and if they are on the run from someone they probably are trying to avoid showing up on paper anywhere. Most lack any sort of job skills, as they have only attended middle or high school infrequently and do not have any marketable skills except their bodies and their youth.

How do homeless kids manage to survive? There are many ways that kids on the streets try to survive and most of these ways are dangerous. The list of options is often lethal and will lead to an early death or to contracting life-threatening diseases.

Homeless teens may engage in prostitution in exchange for money, or informally have sex with strangers in exchange for food or a place to stay even if it is for only a very short period of time, like an hour or a night. For many it is a way to get out of the cold and into an environment that may be warm and even safe. It is sometimes better to be with someone than to be alone on the streets in the middle of winter.

Many panhandle or eat from dumpsters. For some the panhandling is the only way they can get any money to either get out of the cold or to buy drugs or something to eat. Many homeless youth will have figured out where the top restaurants are and will sometime hang out outside the back door as a way of getting fed that night. Some will hang out outside grocery stories after closing and will collect any food items that may have expired or produce that is overly ripe but still edible. They may sleep on the streets, on benches, or on the sidewalk; they may stay in "squats"—abandoned buildings that groups of teenagers take over for themselves—or they may "couchsurf" through the homes of friends and acquaintances (zimbio.com 2010).

There are many misconceptions about why people are homeless. The fact is that as many as 3.5 million Americans are homeless each year, more than 1 million of which are children.

Many people think that most of the homeless are repeating a cycle of homelessness. However, the fact is that more than half of the homeless are families with children who were forced into homelessness by one or more unexpected life altering events. "For example, the loss of loved ones, job loss, domestic violence, divorce, family disputes, depression, untreated mental illness, post-traumatic stress disorder, and physical disabilities"(Eugenia Berezina, 2003).

Homelessness influences every facet of a child's life from conception to young adulthood. The cycle begins early for some and never truly ends, as the child or youth is unable to get out of the cycle because the parent is unable to provide the necessary resources. The experience of homelessness often will inhibit the physical, emotional, cognitive, social, and behavioral development of children because the child is unable to get the proper nutrition, health care, bonding, stimulation, and proper day-to-day care and interaction.Young children are especially vulnerable because when their parents become homeless these children are often separated from their parents by social welfare agencies, which can cause long-term negative effects and post-traumatic stress disorder. "Homeless preschool age children also are more likely to experience major developmental delays and to suffer from emotional problems. Despite these developmental delays and emotional difficulties, homeless pre-schoolers receive fewer services than other children their age" (Eugenia Berezina, 2003).

By the time homeless children reach school age, their homelessness affects their social, physical, and academic lives. Children are very aware of the fact that they are different from their school peers. They are unable to achieve due to the stress of not having the basics to survive. These homeless children are not simply at risk; the majority of them suffer specific physical (lack of developing physically and growing according to developmental milestones; psychological (unable to develop positive images of self, positive cognitive processing and problem solving; and emotional damage (lack of trust, insecurity, hopelessness, depression, increased anxiety) due to the circumstances that accompany episodes of homelessness.

In general, homeless children consistently exhibit more health problems than housed poor children. The lack of medical care and attention will lead to children not receiving the proper immunizations, follow-up care, infections that are treated and can lead to lifelong health problems.

Environmental factors contribute to homeless children's poor health, and homeless children are at high risk for infectious disease. Homeless children are at greater risk for asthma and lead poisoning, often with more severe symptoms than housed children. Many of these children, when they do find housing or shelter, discover that these places are subpar in quality and often found to be infested with other problems like rats and other pests that create health issues.

Poor nutrition also contributes to homeless children's poor health, causing increased rates of stunted growth and anemia. Despite these widespread health problems, homeless children generally lack access to consistent health care, and this lack of care can increase severity of illness. "Homeless children are not simply at risk; most suffer specific physical, psychological, and emotional damage"(Eugenia Berezina, 2003). This result is predictable and is seen as a regular occurrence.

Nongovernment organizations employ a wide variety of strategies to address the needs and rights of street children. The following interventions can be categorized as follows:

Advocacy—through media and government contacts, agencies may press for the rights of street children to be respected. This is often not effective but does bring awareness to the plight of these children. It allows communities to become more aware of what is happening in their own backyards and to seek out some level of support.

Preventive—programs that work to prevent children from taking to the streets, through family and community support and education. The programs of prevention are often underfunded and are reactive in nature. Sometimes it is not till the family or the youth has no other option that they will be able to receive some help. The goal of these programs are good but often they are not fast enough in acting to provide the necessary supports.

Institutional—Residential rehabilitation programs—some agencies provide an environment isolated from the streets where activities are focused on assisting children to recover from drug, physical, or sexual abuse. These institutions have a mandate to provide services but often are overcrowded and there are long waiting lists. There is a great need for these programs but government funding is often minimal or nonexistent. There needs to be more funding allocated to the promotion and maintenance of these programs so as to be able to reach as many individuals as possible within a geographical region.

Full-care residential homes, often the final stage in many agencies' programs, take in the child when he or she is no longer in the streets but lives completely in an environment provided by the agency. The goal of getting all kids off the street is achieved. Some agencies promote fostering children to individual families who either have the formal training as foster parents or are approached on an emergency basis to provide care.

In some states, depending on the numbers of homeless youth, the local agency will set up group homes where a small number of children live together with house parents employed by the agency. In many states there is a grouping of homeless children that are set up in institutional care centers catering to large numbers of children. This solution is becoming less and less as the agencies are not able to keep these large institutions running profitably and are huge drains to the local economy.

Some agencies include a follow-up program that monitors and counsels children and families after the child has left the residential program. There is much variance depending on which state the child lives in, as there are many states that do not have the financial capability to provide this type of support structure. It is an important goal to provide the necessary counseling and therapeutic interventions, but it is often not followed through or sustained with any level of fidelity.

Street-based programs work to alleviate the worst aspects of street life for children by providing services to them in the streets. These programs tend to be less expensive and serve a larger number of street children than institutional programs since the children still must provide for themselves in the streets. These programs will include the following:

Food program: Children and youth receive daily food that is prepared by local agencies or soup kitchens.

Medical services: Youths are given free medical care to address any issues. They may be tested for HIV-AIDS, or sexually transmitted diseases and the appropriate medical interventions. Youths may also receive any needed medications that are needed for daily functioning.

Legal assistance: Many youths are often involved with petty crimes and receive necessary representation if apprehended by the law.

Street education: Counselors will give the youth instruction on how to survive the nasty individuals who cruise for the youths for sex, drugs, or crime. It is a course in street smarts.

Financial services (banking and entrepreneur programs): Since many of the homeless-street youth have never learned to manage their finances beyond spending everything they have every day, this information enables the youth to learn new skills and possibly save enough money to get off the streets.

Family reunification: This is available for those who may want to reunite with their families. However, the reality is that many of these youths have escaped very unpleasant situations and never use this service. There are some happy stories of youths who have been reunited successfully.

Drop-in centers/night shelters: These are used as a way for kids to feel safe and connect to other individuals, especially at night when they are the most vulnerable. For some of these youths these shelters represent the only connection they have to healthy adults and oftentimes will make connections with other street youth and form a circle of protection.

Outreach programs are designed to bring the children into closer contact with the agency and provide them with a variety of services to get them off the streets and back into healthy and protected settings.

Conscientization is the concept that enables a possible change in street children's attitudes to their circumstances, so instead of viewing themselves as an oppressed minority and becoming protagonists, rather than passive recipients of aid, they can become empowered to find solutions that will change the direction of their young lives. This education of these youths enables them so that they can become independent and fully functioning members of the society in which they reside in.

Many agencies employ several of these strategies and a child will pass through a number of stages before he or she "graduates." First he/she will be contacted by individuals in the programs who will encourage the youth to become connected to a drop-in center programs, though still living in the streets. It may be a first step in getting kids off the streets. Later the child may be accepted into a halfway house and finally into residential care where he or she becomes fully divorced from street life (Wikipedia, 2010).

Several studies have explored the issues surrounding family reunification with homeless youths. One such study discussed the program, "Operation Runaway," which based its success with this population according to three basic factors: the model is family focused, crisis oriented, and community based" (D. B. Riley, 2004).

Another critical element of the program explored within this study was the unique partnership between the police and the organization in question. One issue that is mentioned within this area of research is the need for cultural sensitivity when working with families of runaway/homeless youths. After providing a generic model for intervention services, the authors did state that there were risk factors associated with family reunification for runaways. "Parental relationships must be the primary target for interventions. Interventions must include parent training that improves communication and positive parent-child interactions" (D. B. Riley, 2004).

Teaching parents management skills, such as effective parental monitoring and discipline, is needed. Many parents do not have the necessary skill to prevent the youth from leaving again. Parents of these youths are often helpless at coming up with solutions to address the behavior of their teen. Many of them just do not know what to do and therefore need to be guided through the process by counselors and therapists who understand family systems.

Cultural differences in parenting practices among ethnic groups must be addressed prior to reunifying the youth. Specialists who are working in the reunification must have a solid understanding of the culture the youth is from. Parents will relate much better to someone who understands and can support the necessary learning for that family. "Interventions to assist families and youth overcome conflict and rebuild relationships must be culturally sensitive to the divergent needs of these groups" (S. J. Thompson, 2003).

One of the often-discussed means by reestablishing contact between a street youth and his/her family is through the use of a telephone helpline. In one study, the author explored the Message Home Helpline, which is a national free phone helpline available to people who have runaway or left home. This helpline allows them to send a message to their families, to seek confidential advice and if necessary, to be helped to a place of safety (F. Mitchell, 2003).

It was found that the youths in the study called the service within a short time of leaving home. It was determined that this initial contact was critical for youths who wanted to make contact or return to their homes but were afraid to make that initial step. According to the author, "using the helpline to broker that initial contact allowed them to voice their fears and apprehensions and in many cases this facilitated their return home."

As with other interventions, studies suggest that a "one-type, fits-all" model is not effective. In discussing three categories of runaway youths (i.e., runaway-homeless youths, throwaway youths, and independent youths), the authors of the study, "Differences and Predictors if Family Reunification among Subgroups of Runaway Youths Using Shelter Services," revealed that "predictors associated with family reunification among the three subgroups add support for considering key developmental tasks when designing interventions that can affect the experiences of these troubled youths. Intervention

efforts must be based on adequate assessments so that they can be tailored
to the specific needs of these subgroups of youths (S.J. Thompson, 2001)
(Streetconnect.org).

There are a variety of research studies that were conducted in the last several years that recommend general interventions for street kids throughout
North America. Studies involved interviewing both street youth and service
providers as a way to truly identify the needs of that key population. Many
of the street youth interviewed were either living on the street, residing in a
shelter, or using shelter services (such as drop-ins), or had exited street life.

A significant number of the studies involved crisis shelters which provided
short-term services, such as food, health care, etc. It seemed that adolescents
as young as 12 and as old as 23 were the subjects of the majority of the
studies. This range provided a variety of data and information that could be
generalized across states and communities.

The overwhelming and critical finding of these "general" studies was the
need for comprehensive service provision and, similarly, a repeated need for
a coordinated system of care amongst service providers. For example, one
particular study discusses the development of a "dynamic model" which,
according to its author, ". . . provides common ground upon which practitioners, administrators, policy makers, and research communities can consider
the impact and effectiveness of policy and service" (K.M. Staller, 2004).

Another study provided concrete examples of coordination amongst service providers in this area (R.A. Brooks, 2004). For instance, it was noted
that some of the agencies serving street youth would schedule their hours of
operation specifically when other agencies were closed in order to provide a
continuum of services to these youth. There was advocacy for standards of
care (i.e., best practices) to be developed so that the service sector could be
effectively evaluated. The need for comprehensive services was highlighted
in the article entitled "Familial backgrounds and risk behaviors of youth with
thrownaway experiences by C. Wingwalt that was published in 1988. It is
now 2011 and still these comprehensive services are inconsistent and often
unavailable because of lack of support personnel or economic hardships.

It was noted that "thrownaway" youth who demonstrate high-risk behaviors
(e.g., attempting suicide, using substances, etc.) and have familial problems
have a high need for comprehensive services such as intensive counseling
and drug treatment or intervention services that are flexible, coordinated,
community-based continuum of immediate, intermediate, and long-term care to
provide for the basic needs, psychological growth, and career development of
homeless youths (Problems of Homeless Youth, Social Work Vol. 36, 1991).

Critical finding within the research is that services must be tailored to the
youth's individual needs and circumstances, otherwise the time is not well

spent. The youth will often not participate or attend any of the services. In fact they may become very good at avoiding all contact whatsoever and will still be out on the streets.

One recent study done in 2007 entitled "Stories of Working with Homeless Youth "expresses the need for service providers to be highly versatile and recognize the youths' diverse circumstances and tailor "means of engagement and expectations in ways that recognize the unique challenges of homelessness and the pasts that put them on the street. To connect the worker needs to listen, value, not judge, respect, and like youths who have experienced very little of any of these things" (S.A. Kidd 2007).

S.A. Kidd has identified the key to success: it is take the kid from where they are and help them get to a better place. A homeless youth will not leave the streets just because it is the right thing to do, or because someone wants them to; it will be on their time and when they are motivated to do so.

Much of the specific research has focused on examining the personal strengths of youth, and particular attention has been paid to the ways in which the street youth have used informal and formal resources to survive street life. The goal of the researchers is to clearly identify the function of the behavior that may have led to the running away or the situations that resulted in homelessness.

Survival strategies are routinely considered, including, "survival sex" and "squeegeeing." A major theme within a number of these studies is the issue of "coping." One particular study highlighted the development of "street smarts" by homeless youth as a means by which these youth are able to survive on the street (K. Bender, 2007). There are varying levels of coping, and often many of these youths are one hair away from a mental breakdown or suicide, or they have adapted so well that they are now pros at surviving the streets. They have earned their badge of honor on how to beat the next guy and get ahead to live and survive another day.

In terms of service provision, people advocate that practitioners use a "strengths perspective" in order to ". . . empower their clients to become masters of their own lives." The study suggests that ". . . effective programs are those that target the skills and capabilities of those served and offers providers a means to engage these youth that does not involve acting as quasi-parents or guardians" (S.J. Thompson, 2004). The mistake that many service providers make is that they want to rescue these youths. This mistake may cause them the loss of an opening into this youth's life. One should never assume that someone will want a service just because it is good for them. The marketing of the service needs to be youth focused and desirable.

One of the key components in terms of service provision is the importance of valuing and respecting the street youth in a way that helps the youth keep some semblance of dignity. The service providers must be mindful of providing safe and respectful environments that are inviting and welcoming to all youths no matter what experiences they have on the street.

"Critical service delivery components include counseling, life-skills training, job creation, peer support, family therapy, and child care. Education is repeatedly mentioned as a crucial aspect of support services" (S.J. Thompson, 2004). It is a known fact that without these services the likelihood of returning to the streets is a very high certainty.

Early Intervention is cited as critical in service delivery programs (i.e., before the youth becomes firmly entrenched in street life and before a permanent break from family is made). Early Intervention is so important and often does not occur because our society is so reactive and not proactive. In fact, families do not receive any help unless they are in crisis.

When interventions with street youth are made, child- or youth-centered approaches are the preferred method of service delivery because without taking the youth's specific needs into account, the intervention will often fall short or miss the target behavior it is trying to resolve. An important component of support to street youth involves family intervention; in particular, in cases of physical and sexual abuse, there is a very specific need for strengthening family relationships and giving them the skills necessary to begin rebuilding their lives. The abuse did not just develop overnight. It is often a case of many years and sometimes cycles within families that have gone unbroken.

As one study notes: "shelters are required to focus on reunification of youths with their parent(s)." This uninformed general policy may place these youth at further risk for future victimization. It is crucial that the personnel involved in the reunification are aware of all the dynamics that have contributed to the youth leaving home and to be vigilant as to what the additional services are needed, to seeking out the supports and services that are not provided, and to aid in the reunification process. Knowing what is needed and not needed will prevent the possibility of victimization of youth. Knowing and providing after-care services, such as family-oriented interventions to support youth and their parents, may be particularly valuable in successful, long-term reunification (S.J. Thompson 2004).

In terms of the research regarding service provision for street youth, a majority of the studies involve the street youth themselves and "participatory action research" is repeatedly mentioned in the literature. Giving a voice to street youth is often mentioned as important for both service delivery programs and research projects. It is necessary to give voice to those living the nightmares of being on the street. One cannot dismiss or discount the value of a firsthand experience.

For instance, one study highlights the numerous opportunities for street youth to make contributions to programs that they are an integral part of by including them in deciding on a name or choosing an emblem or logo for the program. Youths can be encouraged to decorate and maintain their living space (V. Veeran, 2004). The goal is to give them a sense of ownership and pride in being part of something that is a collective identity.

A number of the studies call for further research in order to examine the most effective services for street youth, both long- and short-term. One of the particular issues regarded as important in this area of research includes the ethical considerations regarding adolescent consent. (www.streetconnect.org 2010).

The following was found online. It is a whole website devoted to Survival of Homelessness. It is written by an individual who has experience in many facets of that life on the street. Here is an excerpt of one of his blogs. (http://guide2homelessness.blogspot.com/2004/12/message-to-homeless-teens.html). His name is Michael C. Benson, and he has asked to be recognized for his life experience. His email address is homelessness@gmail.com.

A Message to Homeless Teens—Blog Spot

If you are a runaway in the United States, unless you have gone through a very difficult procedure to become emancipated, you don't have the right to work or make contacts. This puts you in the worst possible position, a position of artificial dependency, partnered with inexperience and physical awkwardness. You are in trouble.

It may seem that you have four choices: seeking charity, thievery, drug trafficking, or prostitution. Not one of these is an acceptable or sustainable lifestyle, but you may decide to try one or all of them. If you do, know this, it does not make you a beggar, a thief, a drug dealer, or a prostitute. You are who you are, the fiery, self-reliant individual who is aware that he/she has a right to be treated better than what was happening at home. You stood up for yourself, and now I want you to remember that you are worth standing up for. What you are driven to do by need is not who you are. You will prove that later in life. Believe it now.

I want you to think about your troubles one at a time. You must address the same needs an adult has, but you must do it with fewer social resources. You may not be able to get a car, so now think. Where will you find shelter? Consider abandoned buildings. Consider tent living at campsites or in national parks. Consider unused warehouses. Try to avoid people who will give you a place to live in exchange for sex. These relationships almost always end in violence. Getting a place for a night or two is one thing. Getting ensnared long term grows ugly quickly. It is often possible to sleep on buses or subways. Bring a newspaper and hold it up in front of you while you doze off if transit police check for people sleeping. How will you keep warm? Layers of clothing are very helpful. I recently heard an interesting suggestion from polar explorers. If the night is very cold, eat some butter or margarine. This keeps explorers warm in Antarctica, so it is worth considering. Blankets are good. Huddle up with other runaways, if you can find some to get friendly with. They are least likely to exploit you.

Know that you will be exploited, you will be stolen from, you will be victimized. Be at peace with that reality, and try to limit the damage. Try not to get hurt. Never seek revenge. This advice is not applicable to the jail or prison environment where an early show of violent strength may be critical to reducing danger in the future.

Do not use drugs. Please. Just don't do it. This is the time when you will become an addict, because life sucks, and drugs are such an easy and available escape. You must avoid this trap, or you will be paying for it for years to come.

You must survive till you're able to make some contacts, or get involved in the underground economy. You may be able to find work by making friends with Latino day laborers. They often know people who will employ you without documents. Try to obtain false documents that will establish your age at 18 or 19. If you succeed at this, buy a car at your first opportunity and follow the rest of my advice as if you were an adult. If you follow this path, you may take a great deal of pride in how you lived through being a runaway.

The most important thing I can teach is that this will change. Things will get better. Have fun every day. It will help you think. Do something silly. Each day you will find new solutions. Beware of people who want to take over responsibility for your life. What they offer is seldom worth what they want in return.

posted by Mobile Homemaker @ 1:01 PM Survival Guide to Homelessness 2004.

There are many agencies that are focused on ending homelessness in youth. Many of these agencies preach that to end youth homelessness we need to focus on the following ten areas:

10 Needs to Prevent & End Youth Homelessness

- *Plan:* strategies focused on ending youth homelessness
- *Data:* how many youth are homeless, what their needs are, etc.
- *Emergency prevention:* crisis counseling, family reunification services, etc.
- *Systems prevention:* mainstream programs that provide care and services to youth
- *Outreach:* programs that reduce barriers and encourage homeless youth to enter the system

- *Youth housing continuum:* youth shelters, transitional housing, etc.
- *Services:* access to funded services through mainstream programs
- *Youth development:* programs that engage youth in meaningful ways, building leadership and decision-making skills
- *Permanent housing:* supportive housing for homeless youth
- *Income:* assistance to homeless youth to secure income; educational and vocational programs (www.youthnoise.com)

The fact that these have been highlighted does not mean that they will appear. Governments and communities must focus their attention and money to solving these issues, as it will get more drastic every year. The more the economy and social services do not meet the needs of families and youth the more we will see youth becoming homeless and on the street. This issue of street and homeless kids is a solvable issue, it is also preventable.

Why do we need to solve youth homelessness? The broad and complex issue of youth homelessness occupies a place scattered with some of the most persistent problems on the policy landscape. Addiction, homelessness, income inequality, unemployment, malnutrition, mental health issues, physical, sexual, and emotional abuse, youth violence, early school leaving, and teen pregnancy are just some of the complex issues faced by homeless youth.

The social and economic cost to addressing youth homelessness will increase, the numbers of street-involved youth will continue to accelerate, and associated health care, criminal justice, social services and emergency shelter costs will continue to grow. We cannot afford not to make a commitment and be motivated to ending youth homelessness. We are throwing away many young lives that could be valuable resources.

It costs an estimated $30,000—$40,000 per year to keep a youth in the shelter system. The cost of keeping one youth in detention is estimated at over $250 a day, or $100,000 a year (Raising the Roof, 2008). We need to go into action to solve these social issues.

There is a path out of homelessness and it is built upon the foundation of providing stable arrangements for affordable and supportive housing. It is imperative that education, training, and employment be part of any plan. Without these three things youths cannot gain a sense of independence and financial stability to get beyond the survival mode. We need to fill their minds and their wallets so that they become productive members of the community they live in.

Youth who are wrapped up in the cycle of homelessness require reliable and uninterrupted provision of services to address a complex array of issues from physical basics to mental health supports and services. Stability on the part of the service providers is critical if youth are to be allowed to fail, learn from their mistakes, and try again. They need to have mentors that allow them the opportunity to learn, develop new skills, master a series of basic foundational skills, and give them a toolkit of responses and choices when making day-to-day decisions.

Canada, being a socialized society, decided a long time ago that no citizen shall be left out and not provided for. This includes their homeless youth. In a report entitled Homelessness: The Road to Solutions, published in 2008 by the Raising the Roof organization, they formulated the following plan for the continuum of support services that they believe is required to engage youth and support their transition to stability.

They include:

• Food, shelter, and health care to meet immediate and basic needs
• Safe environment, including drop-in services and emergency shelter
• Education and job training designed specifically to meet their needs, and strategies to provide lifestyle stabilization using intensive models of support
• Social networks (trusted and supportive friends/mentors)
• Employment opportunities
• Harm reduction (Raising the Roof, 2008)

If one takes a closer look at these components one can see that they are very realistic, doable, and can change lives very quickly. They are based on very clear solution-based interventions. These interventions allow the service providers to give support where support is needed. It would be advantageous for the United States to begin the discussions around these interventions and provide the necessary services. Maybe it is time for the United States to take a much closer look at the success that Canada is having in addressing the problems of homeless youths.

Raising the Roof organization has indicated in their publication that if youth are to break out of street life, they require access to a range of opportunities. These include the opportunity to

• Live in safe, secure and affordable accommodation
• Go to school, get training or a job
• Have their needs for stability and support met just like others their age
• Participate in planning their own pathways to success (Raising the Roof, 2008)

We know that, with the right supports, youth can find hope for a better future. Many young people want to get into stable housing and access employment and educational opportunities. They have hopes and dreams for their lives. To move forward with program development and structured opportunities that meet their specific needs, street-involved youth require dedicated resources from all levels of government. This will require a nation-wide commitment to address youth homelessness, not simply as a subset of housing, health, or employment programs, but as a distinct and coordinated policy area supported by local community-based delivery and leadership. With dedicated champions, partners and agencies working together with and on behalf of homeless youth, we can create the systems, supports, and oppor-tunities they need to move beyond the streets. It can be done.

Chapter 9

Alternative Programs and Strategies for Children and Youth

Children come in all shapes and sizes. They have different genetics, and life and school experiences. They are abused, neglected, mentally ill, psychopathic, and sociopathic, as well as having many other clinical diagnoses. Is there a program or a strategy that will work best for these damaged youths? The goal of this chapter is to provide the reader with multiple possibilities that will meet the needs of the children as well as the need of the school, community, or home of the troubled youth and children.

"Preventing delinquency," says Peter Greenwood, "not only saves young lives from being wasted, but also prevents the onset of adult criminal careers and thus reduces the burden of crime on its victims and on society." He goes on to say that, "it costs states billions of dollars a year to arrest, prosecute, incarcerate, and treat juvenile offenders. Investing in successful delinquency-prevention programs can save taxpayers seven to ten dollars for every dollar invested, primarily in the form of reduced spending on prisons" (Peter Greenwood).

His reporting of these statistics indicate a real need for states and federal agencies to really begin looking at what works and what is preventative in terms of keeping kids in schools, off the streets, out of crime and violence, and becoming productive members of society.

The Annie Casey Foundation has been a leader in juvenile reform and has come up with eight core components that a program must have to actually initiate change. The Foundation has given permission for these 8 core components to be reproduced for the discussion in this text.

1. "*Collaboration* between the major juvenile justice agencies, other governmental entities, and community organizations. Without collaboration,

even well designed reforms are likely to flounder or be subverted. A formal structure within which to undertake joint planning and policymaking is essential."

It is impossible for agencies to act in isolation of one another. Resources cannot be taken out of one hand to be given to the other. Politicians in Washington and at the state level must have a common goal and want to solve the problem. Not playing together will only create a variety of tunnels that lead to nowhere. Everyone needs to be committed to serving the needs of this population.

2. "Use of accurate data, both to diagnose the system's problems and proclivities and to assess the impact of various reforms, is critical."

In 2011 it is imperative that all agencies make data-driven decisions. It is irresponsible to make decisions that are not well grounded in research or data collection. What the statistics are saying usually indicate the pulse of the problem. Money and resources need to be allocated according to need and demand. States that show a larger need based on very stable statistics should get additional funding and resources to address these issues.

3. "Objective admissions criteria and instruments must be developed to replace subjective decision making at all points where choices to place children in secure custody are made."

Anytime a child enters the system the evaluation measures that are used for placement or intervention must be based in credible and reliable standards. There needs to be some level of consistency of application and interpretation of the results. It cannot be at the whims of a social worker or a case manager. The decisions made must be based from accurate information gathering and data that supports the hypothesis and the needs.

4. "*New or enhanced non-secure alternatives to detention* must be implemented in order to increase the options available for arrested youth. These programs must be careful to target youth who would otherwise be locked up. Whenever possible, they should be based in neighborhoods where detention cases are concentrated and operated by local organizations."

Jail or detention centers are not always the best place for troubled youth yet more often than not that is where they end up. There needs to be a better triage process that evaluates the potential or risk of a youth becoming an aggressor or a victim in the detention system. Oftentimes putting a vulnerable youth in jail only increases the possibility that they will become hardened and even more aggressive.

5. "*Case processing reforms* must be introduced to expedite the flow of cases through the system. These changes reduce lengths of stay in

custody, expand the availability of non-secure program slots, and ensure that interventions with youth are timely and appropriate."

The backlog in the American youth justice system is atrocious and pitiful. The amount of young people waiting to be arraigned is obscene in many large cities. There are too many clients and not enough courtrooms. A system of triage in the justice system would alleviate this problem and the courts would be freed up to deal with the very serious cases. A complete overhaul needs to be done to move this process forward. Unfortunately, this author is not too optimistic at this time as juvenile justice is very rooted in its old practices and procedures.

6. "*Special detention cases*—for youth in custody as a result of probation violations, writs and warrants, as well as those awaiting placement—must be re-examined and new practices implemented to minimize their presence in the secure facility."

As mentioned in the above paragraph the juvenile justice system needs to become more efficient as handling and processing the cases before the courts. Holding youths in adult jails has been proven to be ineffective and downright dangerous. Many of the youths who are incarcerated become victims of violence. The appropriateness of these types of placements for youths need to be well defined and consistently implemented.

7. "*Reducing racial disparities* requires specific strategies (in addition to those listed above) aimed at eliminating bias and ensuring a level playing field for youth of color. Change in this arena also requires persistent, determined leadership because the sensitive nature of these discussions and changes frequently provoke defensiveness and avoidance."

Youths who are culturally different or part of a minority ethnic group need to be given the right opportunities to succeed like everyone else in America. They need to believe that they are on the same playing field as their Caucasian friends. Discrimination and prejudice in this country has to give way to opportunity for all. Education needs to be of high quality and available. Youth of color need to have a semblance of hope for the future.

8. "*Improving conditions of confinement* is most likely to occur when facilities are routinely inspected by knowledgeable individuals applying rigorous protocols and ambitious standards. Absent of this kind of consistent scrutiny, conditions in secure facilities are unlikely to improve and often will deteriorate" (Casey Foundation).

We cannot for one moment become complacent about the facilities that house our youth. We need to make them places of rehabilitation and change. We must continue to regulate the administration of these facilities so that they are places of humanity and dignity and not places of oppression.

It is important to realize that these core initiatives can only happen if communities make the investment into change. To affect the crime rates, the amount of incarcerations systems must be changed. People in power will need to alter their beliefs and attitudes.

Restorative Justice

A model that has gained favor in both criminal justice and educational system is restorative justice. Restorative justice has roots in tribal cultures throughout the world. Pam Stenheim has stated that "these cultures have long understood that the needs of both the victim and community must be considered and addressed before amends can be made." In her work around restorative justice she emphasizes one basic concept: crime damages people, communities, and relationships.

This model holds that justice should focus on trying to repair any injustices or damages done to an individual person, or to a community. The process of healing can only be accomplished once all parties have begun to build a sense of trust and have a motivation to resolve the issues. In a way, the parties must be prepared to make amends for their actions.

Restorative justice is built upon a community which has a set of standards that are enforceable and can be addressed in the process. The method by which restorative justice is done can include: victim-offender mediation, various community decision-making processes that may include appearance in front of panels, restorative community service (picking up trash, helping the disadvantage, restitution in the form of financial compensation, victim and community impact statements, and victim awareness panels (Pam Stenheim)

Restorative justice redefines the way justice systems addresses the criminal activity or an offense toward someone else. It provides a forum to make people accountable for their actions. It also empowers people to do the right thing to make things good again.

Umbreit (2000) lists specific examples of restorative justice: The following can be used as part of any restorative program:

1. Initiatives such as crime repair crews,
2. victim intervention programs,
3. family group conferencing,
4. victim-offender mediation and dialogue,
5. peacemaking circles,
6. victim panels that address offenders,
7. victim empathy classes for offenders, and
8. victim-directed and citizen-involved community service by the offender.

These programs provide higher levels of victim and offender satisfaction and a greater likelihood of successful restitution completion by the offender than traditional justice programs. "Research has also shown that restorative justice programs reduce fear among victims and decrease the frequency and severity of further criminal behavior among offenders" (Umbreit & Fercello, 1997).

Restorative justice has been found to be very effective within the school systems because it offers a proactive alternative for administrators when addressing the involvement of youth in criminal activity. Rather than immediately expelling or suspending youth from school, which in the past has been the norm and is still common with many school administrators, it gives them the option of offering a different way of making amends.

In the past when a student acted out they were often expelled from schools, which drove them into the juvenile court system and juvenile corrections facilities, never to return to school. For many this meant a return to the streets and a life of petty crime. Restorative justice can be incorporated into school policies and practices and is very commonplace in many of the elementary, middle, and high schools throughout the country. Educators have become aware of the powerful impact and the success of this type of intervention. It has kept youths out of the juvenile justice system.

Restorative justice as a program creates opportunity for dialogue among all that are involved. The time to investigate the situation gives all the members involved the chance to review all of the possible reasons for the behavior or crimes and what may have been a factor in the incident. In the evaluation of the situation the school officials are given the opportunity to see whether the young adult had support needs that were not being met; the behavior was a direct result of these unmet needs. It is also very important to have the dialogue on how to make reparations while helping the young adult to find better alternatives and make better choices in the long run. "Schools can promote care and respect by providing restorative justice processes that allow for differences to be worked through in a constructive manner" (Morrison, 2002).

Wrap-Around Services

According to Leone et al. (2002), "a preferred approach for reducing juvenile delinquency and crime is providing wrap-around services and supports through community-based, family-focused, and prevention-oriented collaboration, rather than incarcerating youth for longer periods of time." Wraparound services are often nonexistent in many communities and are ill defined. These services need to be extremely well coordinated and accessible to be effective.

"Youth with disabilities as well as other youth within the juvenile justice system often need a wide range of individualized support. These services need to be comprehensive, collaborative, and available within the diverse communities and environments where these young adults live." (Pam Stenheim) She goes on to emphasize the need for change in how services are delivered to a very fragile population.

It is a very sad reality that so many youths with special needs find themselves on the wrong side of the justice system. For many, their disabilities are not taken into account when sentencing occurs. The law is very black and white. You do the crime you do the time. Detention centers are the last place that youths with special needs should be. They do not receive the necessary supports and intervention. Many of these youths do not have a rehabilitative experience. In fact, many are tragic statistics.

According to the Office of Juvenile Justice and Delinquency Prevention, in a report that was created in 1998, it was stated that "the most promising methods to prevent and reduce delinquency include addressing both risk factors (elements that increase the likelihood of delinquency) and protective factors (elements that insulate children considered at risk for juvenile delinquency) across numerous areas." Almost 13 years later we are still striving to make progress on these recommendations.

Leone et al. (2002) cite "the need for effective collaboration among key community agencies as a fundamental support for youth at risk for or engaged in violent juvenile behaviors." Almost every report investigated for this book indicated that collaboration among all interested parties was the key to success in any type of planning, service delivery, or intervention.

Their model is based upon public health prevention, focusing on early identification, early intervention after onset, individualized services, and aftercare within collaborative systems of prevention, treatment, and care. It is a model that has been around for 10 years, yet it is still not fully implemented in many communities in America.

Alternative High Schools

The National Crime Prevention Council has put forth the idea that alternative high schools, often called learning academies, can be places of success for troubled youth. These schools are often small-scale school environments where a very limited number of students, sometimes less than 25, receive intensive tutoring, consistent discipline with sanctions, counseling to establish goals for academic success and a transition to work, and guidance on developing life skills to cope with any special needs. These schools are meant to provide services and teaching in an alternative way that meets the needs of the student more concisely than a regular public school might.

The programs are run as separate entities of existing local high schools or as off-site programs (often referred to as the MALL Program) that serve students from several areas in the community or a juvenile court jurisdiction. The alternative schools usually require parents to give permission and at times sign off for their son or daughter to be placed in the environment. It is often presented to the parents as a last hope for their child to get a high school education. The programs can be voluntary or mandatory. If the program is mandatory there is a strong correlation that the youth has been involved with the juvenile justice system in some way (National Crime Prevention Council).

School Resource Officers

Security officers, but most often state or local police officers who have specialize training in youth or gang activities, are a necessary presence on high school campuses throughout American schools. School counselors may also be trained in security, as they are assigned to patrol school buildings during school hours. Their mandate is to develop positive relationships with students and staff, to recognize and respond to security threats on campus, and to deter crime through their visible presence in the school and at school-sponsored activities. They are seen as resources to all within the building. They are often the first line of defense in many conflict situations and can react and defuse situations readily.

The officers may also sponsor or lead specific educational (drug prevention, conflict management) or recreational activities on campus as a means of building positive relationships with students. Some schools have established mentoring programs, pairing school resource officers with students who have discipline problems (National Crime Prevention Council).

Before and After School Programs

Many schools permit children to arrive early, when parents must leave for work, because otherwise the child would be unsupervised and/or alone within the home or the community. Schools have taken advantage of parents working to have children stay late in the afternoon to take advantage of tutoring, athletics, supervised programs, or playtime that builds on academic and social skills for children who may be lacking them.

Before-and afterschool programs are usually run by college-age volunteers, school staff which may include the child's classroom teacher, or organizations willing to conduct programs at schools. They can also be based at community centers or church buildings with the support of the school community and district resources.

It is important that the program not be viewed as a babysitting service or an extension of school time, but rather a time during which children's developmental needs are served. Successful programs provide opportunities for play, creativity, companionship, and relaxation (National Crime Prevention Council).

Training School Personnel in Crime Prevention

The National Crime Prevention Council has developed a very clear and concise program on how to train teachers. This violence prevention training builds the abilities of school personnel to prevent and respond to incidents in the school. Teachers should be trained in the following skills:

- improving the school climate through after-school activities
- conflict mediation
- recognizing the impact of social influences such as poverty and racism on student behavior
- promoting empathy among students for the concerns of others
- helping students control impulses to react violently when challenged
- teaching students problem-solving skills
- communicating with parents to get them to reinforce lessons from the classroom
- building self-esteem in students through praise and recognition
- using and teaching students to use resources in the community to address their needs.

Successful training programs for school staff also include training in implementing and enforcing school disciplinary and security procedures. Uniform application of these rules establishes a standard of behavior in the school and helps protect students, teachers, and staff (National Crime Prevention Council).

The key to success to any violence prevention program is how well the staff that is trained adheres to the guidelines and implements them with fidelity. It is about being accountable and maintaining that high standard that will lead to safe environments for all.

Gun-Free School Zones

Establishing policies prohibiting the possession of guns in schools and in communities goes a long way in preventing many gun-related crimes. Community laws designate school buildings, school bus stops, and the perimeter area around school buildings as weapon-free zones, where possession or use of a firearm, knife, or other weapon carries additional penalties for the offender. In many states it is illegal to possess a weapon if you are a minor.

This strategy aims to deter offenders from carrying and using a gun or knife in the zone by imposing increased penalties. The penalties do not always discourage the youth offender but it may make them think twice about bringing a weapon to school. School and law enforcement officials believe that the policies are very effective in securing areas frequented by school-aged youth and staff while school is in session. It is unfortunate if a youth wants to bring a weapon to school, he can find ways of concealing the weapon and enter the building. By having gun-free zones the discussion has begun and the expectations are put into place to have a safe school.

In addition to enhanced sanctions, most school districts where such policies are in place also have implemented antiviolence and gun education programs to reinforce among students the belief that carrying guns and knives to school is not safe and should not be tolerated by them and by their peers. They have used education and awareness to change attitudes and behaviors (National Crime Prevention Council).

Diversity and Tolerance Education in Schools

Teaching tolerance in elementary schools reduces the incidence of hate crimes, racism, discrimination, and bigotry. Children are aware of racial and gender differences at a very young age, and by age twelve they have formed stereotypes. In fact, recent studies show that tolerance education is most effective between the ages of four and nine years. Therefore, it is important to teach tolerance to young children and continue reinforcing the message over time.

Age-appropriateness is involved in the creation of the different curricula that educators have developed. For instance, part of the curriculum includes classroom exercises from newsletters and newspaper sections directed toward younger audiences. Additional methods include short theatrical productions and role-playing exercises (National Crime Prevention Council).

Program Types

The following programs have been researched and documented by the Office of Juvenile Justice and Delinquency Prevention. Each one of these alternative strategies has been well documented and has proven to be successful with a variety of youth at risk. These strategies have been summarized here for the reader. Extended explanations can be found on the OJJDP website for the interested reader. The following summaries may be found at http://www.ojjdp.gov/mpg/programTypesDefinitions.aspx.

This text has been reproduced with the permission of the OJJDP.

1. Academic Skills Enhancement programs use instructional methods designed to increase student engagement in the learning process and hence increase their academic performance and bonding to the school (e.g., cooperative learning techniques and "experiential learning" strategies).
2. Aftercare is a reintegrative service that prepares out-of-home placed juveniles for reentry into the community by establishing the necessary

collaborative arrangements with the community to ensure the delivery of prescribed services and supervision. A comprehensive aftercare process typically begins after sentencing and continues through incarceration and an offender's release into the community.

3. Afterschool/Recreation programs offer rewarding, challenging, and age-appropriate activities in a safe, structured, and positive environment. They may reduce delinquency by way of a socializing effect through which youth learn positive virtues such as discipline or simply reduce the opportunity for youth to engage in delinquency.

4. Alcohol and Drug Therapy / Education seeks to reduce the use or abuse of illegal drugs or alcohol by educating youth about the effects of drugs/alcohol. Programs in this category may take many forms, including 12-step programs such as Alcoholics Anonymous or Narcotics Anonymous, school-based and community-based prevention programs targeting alcohol, tobacco, or other drug use, and national public awareness campaigns.

5. Alternative School is essentially specialized educational environments that place a great deal of emphasis on small classrooms, high teacher-to-student ratios, individualized instruction, noncompetitive performance assessments, and less structured classrooms. The purpose of these schools is to provide academic instruction to students expelled or suspended for disruptive behavior or weapons possession, or who are unable to succeed in the mainstream school environment.

6. Classroom Curricula are classroom-based instruction programs designed to teach students factual information; increase their awareness of social influences to engage in misbehavior; expand their repertoires for recognizing and appropriately responding to risky or a potentially harmful situation (e.g., drug use, gang involvement, violence); increase their appreciation for diversity in society; improve their moral character; improve conflict resolution skills; and encourage accountability.

7. Cognitive Behavioral Treatment seeks to correct an individual's faulty perceptions of themselves and/or the world around them. This type of therapy provides skills individuals can use to monitor their thought patterns and correct their behavior as situations unfold around them. Treatment may also focus on relapse prevention by having juveniles evaluate situations that may lead to a relapse of delinquent behavior, and then plan for how to either avoid them or to cope with them effectively.

8. Community and Problem-Oriented Policing involves policing strategies designed to prevent crime by reducing opportunities and increasing the risks for engaging in criminal behavior through mutually beneficial ties between police and community members.

9. Community Awareness/Mobilization includes a broad array of community strategies designed to increase the development of broad, community-based crime prevention partnerships; increase public awareness of and support for crime prevention; and increase the capacity of diverse communities to deal with crime and victimization.

10. Conflict Resolution/Interpersonal Skills building refers to a wide range of processes that encourage nonviolent dispute resolution. In general, these processes teach young people decision-making skills to better manage conflict in juvenile facilities, schools, and communities. Youth learn to identify their interests, express their views, and seek mutually acceptable solutions to disputes. Common forms of conflict resolution include: negotiation, mediation, arbitration, community conferencing, and peer mediation. Similarly, interpersonal skill building focuses on developing the social skills required for an individual to interact in a positive way with others. The basic skills model begins with an individual's goals, progresses to how these goals should be translated into appropriate and effective social behaviors, and concludes with the impact of the behavior on the social environment.

11. Correctional Facilities are public or private residential facilities with construction fixtures or staffing models designed to physically restrict the movements and activities of juveniles or other individuals. They are used for the placement, after adjudication and disposition, of any juvenile who has been adjudicated as having committed an offense, or of any other individual convicted of a criminal offense.

12. Day Treatment facilities (or day reporting centers) are highly structured, community-based, post-adjudication, nonresidential programs for serious juvenile offenders. The goals of day treatment are to provide intensive supervision to ensure community safety and a wide range of services to the offender to prevent future delinquent behaviors. The intensive supervision is fulfilled by requiring the offender to report to the facility on a daily basis at specified times for a specified length of time. Generally, programs are provided at the facility during the day and/or evening at least 5 days a week. Special weekend activities may also be conducted.

13. Drug Court is a type of specialty court established within and supervised by juvenile courts to provide specialized services for eligible drug-involved youth and their families. In general, drug courts provide (1) intensive supervision over delinquency and status offense cases that involve substance-abusing juveniles and (2) coordinated and supervised delivery of an array of support services necessary to address the problems that contribute to juvenile involvement in the justice system. The services

typically include: substance abuse treatment, mental health, primary care, family, and education.

14. Family Therapy focuses on improving maladaptive patterns of family interaction and communication. It is typically implemented with youth diagnosed with mild emotional and behavioral problems such as conduct disorder, depression, and school or social problems. The program is usually conducted by trained therapists in clinical settings with the parents and child.

15. Gang Prevention programs can be grouped into one of two categories. The first is gang membership prevention programs that try to prevent youth from joining gangs. The second is gang intervention programs that intercede with existing gang members during crisis conflict situations.

16. Group Home are residential placements for juveniles that operate in a homelike setting in which a number of unrelated children live for varying time periods. Group homes may have one set of house parents or may have a rotating staff. Some therapeutic or treatment group homes have speciallytrained staff to assist children with emotional and behavioral difficulties.

17. Gun Court: A gun court is a type of specialty court that intervenes with youth who have committed gun offenses that have not resulted in serious physical injury. Most juvenile gun courts are short-term programs that augment rather than replace normal juvenile court proceedings.

18. Home Confinement w/without EM or house arrest with and without electronic monitoring (EM) is a community corrections program designed to restrict the activities of offenders in the community. This sanction allows offenders to remain in their homes, go to work, run errands, attend school, and maintain other responsibilities. However, their activities are closely monitored (either electronically and/or by frequent staff contacts) to ensure that they comply with the conditions set by the court. Offenders placed under home confinement are restricted to their residence for varying lengths of time and are required to maintain a strict schedule of daily activities.

19. Leadership and Youth Development programs prevent problems behaviors by preparing young people to meet the challenges of adolescence through a series of structured, progressive activities and experiences that help them obtain social, emotional, ethical, physical, and cognitive competencies. This approach views youth as resources and builds on their strengths and capabilities to develop within their own community. It focuses on the acquisition of adequate attitudes, behaviors, and skills.

20. Mentoring involves a relationship over a prolonged period of time between two or more people where an older, caring, more experienced individual

provides help to the younger person as he or she goes through life. The goal of mentoring is to support the development of healthy individuals by addressing the need for positive adult contact, thereby reducing risk factors and enhancing protective factors for problem behavior.

21. Parent Training programs involve educating parents on specific management skills. This highly structured approach generally includes parents only, in small groups led by a skilled trainer or clinician. The program typically follows a curriculum guide and often includes video presentations of effective and ineffective ways of parenting; short lectures and discussions to identify parenting principles; interactive exercises; role-plays of direct practice in the parenting behavior to be changed; charting and monitoring of parenting and children's behavior, and assignment of homework.

22. Probation Services refer to a variety of probation-oriented programs, including traditional probation, intensive supervision, and school-based probation. Traditional probation is a disposition in which youth are placed on informal/voluntary or formal/court ordered supervision. Intensive supervision programs (ISPs) are community-based, post-adjudication, non-residential programs designed to provide restraints on offenders in the community. School-based probation is a program partnership between juvenile probation departments and local schools that places probation officers directly within the confines of the school.

23. Reentry Court is a specialized court that manages the return of the offender to the community after being released from a residential placement. The court manages reentry by using its authority to apply graduated sanctions and positive reinforcement as well as direct resources to support the offender's reintegration and to promote positive behavior.

24. Residential Treatment Centers (RTCs) are residential treatment facilities offering a combination of substance abuse and mental health treatment programs and 24-hour supervision in a highly structured (often staff-secure) environment. They usually house youth with significant psychiatric or substance abuse problems who have proved too ill or unruly to be housed in foster care, day treatment programs, and other non-secure environments, but who do not yet merit commitment to a psychiatric hospital or secure corrections facility.

    Although such treatment centers must be licensed by the state, they are frequently run by private, for-profit and nonprofit institutions, and the treatment approaches and admissions criteria used by RTCs vary widely from state to state and institution to institution.

25. Restorative Justice is a theory of justice that emphasizes repairing the harm caused or revealed by criminal behavior. Practices and programs reflecting

restorative purposes will respond to crime by 1) identifying and taking steps to repair harm, 2) involving all stakeholders, and 3) transforming the traditional relationship between communities and government in responding to crime. Some of the programs typically associated with restorative justice include: victim offender mediation, conferencing, circles, victim assistance, ex-offender assistance, restitution, and community service.

26. School/Classroom Environment programs seek to reduce or eliminate problem behaviors by changing the overall context in which they occur. These strategies may include interventions to change the decision-making processes or authority structures (building school capacity); redefining norms for behavior and signaling appropriate behavior through the use of rules (setting norms for behavior); reorganizing classes or grades to create smaller units, continuing interaction, or different mixes of students, or to provide greater flexibility in instruction (classroom organization); and the use of rewards and punishments and the reduction of down time (classroom management).

27. Teen/Youth Court (or peer courts) are much like traditional courts in that there are prosecutors and defense attorneys, offenders and victims, and judges and juries, but young people rather than adults fill these roles and, most important, determine the disposition. The principal goal of a teen court is to hold young offenders accountable for their behavior by imposing sanctions that will repair some of the harm imposed on the victim and community.

28. Truancy Prevention is designed to promote regular school attendance through one or more strategies including an increase in parental involvement, the participation of law enforcement, the use of mentors, court alternatives, or other related strategies.

29. Vocational/Job Training programs address youth crime and unemployment by providing participants with social, personal, and vocational skills and employment opportunities to help them achieve economic success, avoid involvement in criminal activity, and subsequently increase social and educational functioning.

30. Wilderness Camps or challenge programs are generally residential placements that provide participants with a series of physically challenging activities, such as backpacking or rock climbing in an outdoor setting. These programs vary widely in terms of settings, types of activities, and therapeutic goals; but their treatment components are grounded in experiential learning, which advocate "learning by doing" and facilitates opportunities for personal growth.

31. Wraparound/Case Management is a system of care that "wraps" a comprehensive array of individualized services and support around youth and their

families to keep delinquent youth at home and out of institutions whenever possible. Treatment services are usually provided by multiple agencies working together as part of a collaborative interagency agreement, and each youth's treatment plan is determined by an interdisciplinary team consisting of a caseworker, family and community members, and several social services and mental health professionals. Individual case management is a less intense form of the wraparound approach where individual caseworkers guide youth through the existing social services or juvenile justice system and ensure that they receive appropriate services (OJJSP, 2010).

Programs for juvenile delinquents have been numerous and available. What about very young offenders? There are children under 12 who are too young to be involved in incarceration or may not have the cognitive ability to truly understand their actions. Recent instances of children committing homicides have come to national attention and have attracted intense media scrutiny.

Despite the nationwide outrage in response to some of these cases, the number of juveniles age 12 or younger who are involved in murder is relatively small. Between 1980 and 1997, about 2 percent (or 600 cases) of murders involved such child offenders, and the annual number of these murders was relatively stable, averaging about 30 per year.

According to the FBI's Supplementary Homicide Reports (Snyder, 2001): The large majority (84 percent) of children who were aggressors and murdered other individual are males. Seventy percent of the murder victims of child delinquents were male and likely to be acquaintances or family members. More than one-half (54 percent) of the murder victims of child delinquents were killed with a firearm. These statistics are both horrendous and totally unnecessary. We need to educate and prevent access to firearms.

"The most promising school and community prevention programs for child delinquency focus on several risk domains" (Herrenkohl et al., 2001). It is important to fully understand the problem before one can address it effectively. These risk domains are great predictors for future violence and acting out on the part of troubled youth.

Several government agencies who are on the front line in dealing with child delinquency recommend integrating the following types of school and community prevention programs.

These additional program recommendations were also highlighted in the Office of Juvenile Justice and Delinquency Programs Report: This text has been reproduced with permission of the OJJDP.

1. Classroom and behavior management programs. Since children spend so much time in the classroom, it is important to structure lessons and

    discussions in a safe environment so that children will learn appropriate behaviors in the correct context.

2. Multi-component classroom-based programs are instrumental in teaching children how to understand their emotions and their behaviors. Within the school environment there are many different areas that can be used to teach the child new skills. The opportunity to generalize their learning is frequent and well monitored.

3. Social competence promotion curriculums empower students to learn new social skills that they can generalize to their everyday life in and out of school. These curriculums can enable the child to role play in a safe environment and learn which skills are the social norms in that community.

4. Conflict resolution and violence prevention curriculums enable children to understand how to regulate and understand their emotions. They become better able to mediate their problems and to learn a system of conflict resolution rather than one based in violence.

5. Bullying prevention programs are nationwide and abundant. There are several programs that recently have focused on teaching and educating both teachers and students on how to prevent bullying, how to report bullying, and how not to be a victim of bullying.

6. After-school recreation programs have been instrumental in guiding children to leave the street and to stay in a protected environment where they are supervised and guided to learn and participate in safe activities. These recreational activities have been known to teach as well as counsel children who are having difficulties.

7. Mentoring programs have given specific vocational and interest-based skills to children who may not have had any type of goal or direction in their life. These programs have exposed and introduced troubled children with hope and promise at having a possible career, or have provided positive adult or youth role models.

8. School organization programs have helped children to have choices to funnel their energy beyond criminal activity. These programs have allowed children to become involved in positive ways and to be connected to their school. It has allowed children to build a sense of school pride and to belong to something that values their participation.

9. Comprehensive community interventions have become important in reclaiming a community from drug- and crime-infested behaviors. The rebirth of some communities by regaining control and driving out the negative factors that could and do influence children to a life of crime have been eradicated and replaced with positive actions and programs that have offered children new options and new hope. Several of these

unique programs have demonstrated that interventions with young children can reduce later delinquency.

10. Common Sense Parenting (CSP) is a group-based parent training class designed for parents of youth ages 6–16 who exhibit significant behavior and emotional problems. The objective of the program is to teach positive parenting techniques and behavior management strategies to help increase positive behavior, decrease negative behavior, and model appropriate alternative behavior for children. The program consists of six weekly 2-hour sessions involving a group of 10–12 parents led by certified trainers who work from a detailed trainer's manual. The session topics are: a-Parents Are Teachers, b-Encouraging Good Behavior, c- Preventing Problems, d-Correcting Problem Behavior, d-Teaching Self-Control, e-Putting It All Together.

Common Sense Parenting classes concentrate on experiential learning and consist of five training components—review, instruction, modeling, practice, and feedback—and conclude with a summary. Each session is designed to teach one parenting concept and a skill related to that concept.

During each training session, parents review the skills learned during the previous session, receive instruction in a new parenting skill, view videotaped models of the new skill, practice how to use the skill in simulated role-play, and receive feedback from the trainer. Parenting skills and techniques are taught to be adapted by parents for use in any home environment. Parents learn skills such as the use of clear communication, positive reinforcements and consequences, self-control, and problem-solving (OJJDP, 2010).

There are additional programs that have also had documented success in dealing with youths that are violent or are involved in criminal activities. This author is not endorsing any of these programs but is providing their program components for reference or information purposes only.

CeaseFire Chicago is a Chicago, Illinois-based violence-prevention program administered by the Chicago Project for Violence Prevention since the program began in 1999. CeaseFire uses an evidence-based public health approach to reduce shootings and killings by using highly trained street violence interrupters and outreach workers, public education campaigns, and community mobilization, rather than aiming to directly change the behaviors of a large number of individuals.

CeaseFire concentrates on changing the behavior and risky activities of a small number of selected members of the community who have a high chance of either "being shot" or "being a shooter" in the immediate future.

The activities of CeaseFire are organized into five core components, which address both the community and those individuals who are most at risk of involvement in a shooting or killing:

1. Street-level outreach: going out in the streets to reach the clients.
2. Public education: in multiple forms to build knowledge and skills
3. Community mobilization: get everyone in the community to care and get involved
4. Faith leader (clergy) involvement: gives a sense of faith and moral guidance
5. Police and prosecutor participation: get everyone involved in the juvenile system to become stakeholders.
   (http://www.ojjdp.gov/mpg/mpgProgramDetails.aspx?ID=835)

CeaseFire's interventions are based on a theory of behavior that specifies the information data that needs to be assembled and set in motion and how they cause the "outcomes," including reductions in shootings and killings. Many of the program's daily activities target the causal factors linking inputs to outcomes, which were presumed to be among the major determinates of violence. The research this program has done has discovered that there are several causal factors that are believed to contribute to violence. They may include but are not limited to the community norms that are the standard expectation, availability of on-the-spot alternatives for youth to be involved in or have access to, instead of resorting to violence when the situation arises, and the youth's awareness of the risks and costs associated with violence.

First, the program aims at changing the local norms regarding violence. They begin by working in both the wider community and among its clients through a variety of ways. This may include trying a community mobilization where community members are made aware of the issues and concerns. It may be a well-defined public education campaign that targets core parts of the community. It may be through mentoring efforts of outreach workers who are calculated to influence beliefs about the appropriateness of violence. It may begin with conversations one on one. Outreach workers are charged with stimulating a level of change among clients and guiding them toward alternatives rather than using violence or shootings as a way of solving problems. It provides the youth with some level of choice and education about making informed and appropriate decisions.

Outreach workers counsel a small group of young clients, who are recruited from the streets and not through institutions, and connect them to a range of services. The reason for this is to have youths talk to other youths. It has been proven that kids listen to other kids if they believe the youth has credibility through their experiences.

Workers also conduct a significantly high number of conflict mediations as a way to model problem-solving strategies and positive resolution for conflict that does not involve violence. The efforts of the clergy and residents of the community are also aimed primarily at norm change, both in the community and among clients of the outreach workers and other high-risk youth.

Community involvement also targets the perceived costs of violence. People become informed through very specific data and evidence. The public education campaign is aimed at both changing norms about violence and enhancing the perceived risks of engaging in violence. It gives a realistic perspective of the overall costs of violence in a community.

Second, the program provides on-the-spot alternatives to violence when gangs and individuals on the street are making behavior decisions. This program is in the streets and present. Concerned persons are there to act when needed. The program treats young people as rational actors capable of making choices, and the strategy is to promote their consideration of a broader array of response to situations that too often elicit shootings and killings as a problem-solving tactic. The expression of respect and problem-solving mediation techniques are shown to be effective and can be better choices than extreme violence.

Violence interrupters work on the streets alone or in pairs to mediate conflicts between gangs and stem the cycle of retaliatory violence that threatens to break out following a shooting. It provides an alternative to just going out and killing for revenge.

Violence interrupters work the street in the night talking to gang leaders, distraught friends and relatives of recent shooting victims, and others who are positioned to initiate or sustain cycles of violence. Their presence is a positive resource available to youths to explore their options and make a better choice.

Finally, the program aims to increase the perceived risks and costs of involvement in violence among high-risk, largely young people. This reflects a classic deterrence model of human behavior, with risks such as incarceration, injury, and death highlighted for youth. Actions by the police and prosecutors, as well as tougher antigun legislation, are seen as targeting the risks surrounding involvement in shootings (OJJDP, 2010).

Family Centered Treatment (FCT) is a treatment model designed for use in the provision of intensive in-home services. FCT is especially well suited for high-risk juveniles who are not responding to typical community-based services or who have been found to need institutional placement, as well as those returning from incarceration or institutional placement.

A primary goal of FCT is to keep the youth in the community and divert them from further penetration into the juvenile justice system. FCT is different from other traditional in-home family therapy or counseling programs in that it is family focused rather than client focused. Treatment services concentrate on providing a foundation that maintains family integrity, capitalizes on the youth's and family's inherent resources (i.e., skills, values, and communication patterns), develops resiliency, and demands responsibility and accountability.

FCT was first develop because practitioners wanted to have at their disposal simple, practical, and commonsense solutions for families faced with forced removal of their children from the home or dissolution of the family. Oftentimes the removal was due to external and internal stressors and circumstances that were often unclear or confusing to the parents.

The basic framework for treatment draws from components of evidence-based models such as Eco Structural Family Therapy developed by Aponte in 1976 and Emotionally Focused Therapy developed by Johnson and Greenberg in 1985. These individuals were the front runners and pioneers in trying to solve the problem.

FCT is a model of treatment that integrates behavioral change with a primary emphasis on value change for the members of the system. A fundamental premise of FCT is that youth and their families' long-term changes are predicated upon their valuing the changes made, because changes made for compliance or conformity are not sustainable after treatment ends.

Program services include case management, supervision, group meetings, outreach services, crisis prevention/intervention services, and community services. Treatment is conducted in natural settings (i.e., in the home, school, or community), and typically lasts about 6 months, with several hours of contact in multiple sessions every week. FCT is structured into four phases:

1. Joining and Assessment. The Family Centered Specialist (FCS) engages and gains acceptance by the family and works with them to identify areas that affect their functioning.
2. Restructuring. The FCS and family use experiential practice to alter ineffective behavioral patterns among family members. This process includes techniques to modify the crisis cycle to more adaptive patterns of family functioning.
3. Value Change. Through powerful emotional intervention techniques, family members integrate new behaviors into their personal value systems to create long-term change. Giving to others or back to the community is integral in this phase.
4. Generalization. With new skills for dealing with conflict and increased understanding of its own dynamics, the family continues its work, but the treatment is less intense and frequent. The focus is on practice, review of what has worked previously, and reversals (OJJDP, 2010).

The model allows the flexibility to move back and forth between the restructuring and value change phases in order to respond to individual family dynamics. The FCS transitions the family from one phase into the next phase as the family demonstrates behaviors reflective of the key indicators of change (OJJDP, 2010).

Preparing for the Drug Free Years (PDFY), a program for parents of children in grades 4 through 8, was developed by Hawkins and Casatelon whose main goal was to design a program that reduced adolescent drug use and behavior problems. PDFY's skill-based curriculum enables parents to identify and address risks that can and often will contribute to drug abuse while trying to strengthen family bonding by building protective factors like trust, awareness and relationship building.

PDFY is well embedded in the social development model, which emphasizes that young people should experience opportunities for active involvement in the family where they are involved and connected to these individuals. Young people in schools should feel protected. When in their community they should be able to be functioning members and develop skills for success, and should be given recognition and reinforcement for positive effort and improvement.

PDFY focuses on strengthening family bonds and establishing clear standards for behavior that are clearly articulated and defined. This creates a plan to help parents manage their child's behavior while encouraging their development. The ultimate goal of PDFY is to reach parents before their children begin experimenting with drugs. The core curriculum of the family sessions is to focus and build family relationships and communication where specific skills are taught, reinforced, and practiced with a certain amount of success.

The curriculum also helps parents to build their family management skills such as giving directions and commands, requests, and follow through when dealing with difficult situations. Since many parents do not have a skill set around resolution of family conflict, they are coached on how to deal effectively with conflict that leads to successful resolution rather than additional conflict (Hawkins &Casatelon, 1999).

The HOMEBUILDERS Program is one of the best documented Intensive Family Preservation Programs in the country. The program is designed to break the cycle of family dysfunction by strengthening families, keeping children safe, and preventing foster care, residential, and other forms of out-of-home placement. This program's main goal is to build family engagement, and to support and keep families together as much as possible. It is a lofty goal but is doable and realistic.

The program goals have clearly been articulated and developed. They may include some or all of the following as part of the individual and family program. Each individual family's plan may include improving family functioning; increasing social support; increasing parenting skills; preventing or reducing child abuse and neglect; improving school and job attendance and performance; improving household living conditions; establishing daily routines; improving adult and child self-esteem; helping clients become self-directed; and enhancing motivation for change while decreasing family conflict and other problems.

The program values the importance of meeting and taking parents and family units in their present circumstances, and building the necessary skills that will lead to a more successful family unit. The program is designed for the most seriously troubled families, especially those that have experienced assault, abuse, and neglect and even victimization—those who are referred by a number of child service agencies. Populations served include newborns to teenagers and their families. If the family is in crisis there is a very good possibility that they will qualify.

The program includes 4–6 weeks of intensive, in-home services to children and families. A practitioner with a caseload of two families provides counseling, hard services, develops community support, and spends an average of 8–10 hours per week in direct contact with the family, and is on call 24 hours a day, seven days a week for crisis intervention. There is always a back-up team to provide the necessary support and intervention when needed.

The program utilizes a single practitioner model with a team backup for cotherapy and consultation. Teaching strategies involve modeling, descriptions of skills and behaviors, role plays, and rehearsals of newly acquired skills. Teaching tools include skills-based video- and audio-tapes, workbooks, handouts, articles, and exercises. "Therapeutic processes used are skill building, behavioral interventions, motivational interviewing, relapse prevention, rational emotive therapy, and other cognitive strategies" (Charlotte Booth, 1999).

In the last few years Diversion programs have become very popular in many states as a way of dealing with juvenile offenders. Diversion is "an attempt to divert, or channel out, youthful offenders from the juvenile justice system" (Bynum and Thompson, 1996:430). "The concept of diversion is based on the theory that processing certain youth through the juvenile justice system may do more harm than good" (Lundman, 1993).

The basis of the diversion argument is that courts may stigmatize some youth for having committed relatively petty acts that might best be handled outside the formal system. Not all youths need to come in front of a court of law. It is not the best use of court or justice time. In part, diversion programs are also designed to ameliorate the problem of overburdened juvenile courts and overcrowded corrections institutions (including detention facilities), so that courts and institutions can focus on more serious offenders.

Goals and Objectives of Diversion Programs

The major goals of the program are to reduce the number of youth in court-ordered detention and provide youth with culturally relevant community-based services and with supervision. Diversion program provides an intensive level of community-based monitoring and advocacy not available within the traditional juvenile justice system.

Specific Diversion program objectives include the following:

- Ensuring that a high proportion of program clients are not rearrested while participating in the program.
- Ensuring that youth appear in court as scheduled.
- Reducing the population of the Youth Guidance Center (the juvenile court), currently the only place of juvenile detention in the city.
- Providing interventions for youth diverted from secure detention facilities.
- Demonstrating that community-based interventions are an effective alternative to secure custody and can meet the needs of both the youth and the community at a cost savings to the public.
- Reducing disproportionate minority incarceration (including detention) (CJCJ, 2010).

There is still some additional research that needs to be conducted on the effectiveness of Diversion programs. The goals are the pathways to changing how we deal with youth offenders. There has to be a better way because what we have been doing for decades is not working.

Youth Advocate Programs, Inc. (YAP) provides a community-based alternative to placement for Juvenile Probation Departments. The goals and mission of this program is a strength-based, family-focused program that serves adjudicated juvenile offenders whose behavior and social circumstances put them at risk of placement in residential facilities. Many of these youths would not survive or would be attacked and assaulted within an institution or a juvenile detention center. Eligible youth are those deemed by the courts to be in need of residential care for a multiple reasons that are assessed and part of the evaluation report. The program follows an innovative advocacy/wraparound model that includes a comprehensive mix of highly individualized services for youth and their families. The program goals are to:

- Decrease the occurrence of juvenile crime and enhance community safety;
- Increase opportunities for success and improve quality of life for youth and families; and
- Facilitate community empowerment (Youth Advocate Program)

YAP today provides programs for high-risk youth and their families in Texas, Florida, South Carolina, New York, New Jersey, Ohio, Pennsylvania, Arizona, Louisiana, and the District of Columbia (Youth Advocate Program)

The S.T.A.R. Program

The program is used by schools and juvenile judges as an alternative to suspension, expulsion out of school detention and other more expensive and less effective disciplinary tools. Students placed in the Student Transition and Recovery Program are required to attend their normal classes at their normal schools and return home each evening. In the morning before school and in the afternoon after school, students participate in exercises, counseling, tutoring, and military-style drills. Throughout the school day S.T.A.R. Instructors check on the students in their classes and during lunch to ensure appropriate behavior. The youths in this program are monitored frequently and made accountable for their behavior no matter where they are. There is no escaping or avoiding accepting responsibility.

This program has been grouped in the Boot Camp list of alternatives. This type of program has had several controversies attached to it and has been found to be abusive in some areas of the United States. However, some of these programs have had remarkable successes with at-risk youth. It was included in this section for information purposes only.

The Mountain Homes Youth Ranch Program is divided into three phases and is defined by specific benchmarks that need to be accomplished at each stage. In the Beginning phase, participants learn the interdependency of nature's resources, personal skill and knowledge, and responsible and cooperative behavior for the sustaining of life's basic needs. They become tuned to what nature can offer as part of a recovery program. They become more aware of themselves and their environment. As participants learn ancient Indian skills using the resources of nature, they begin to develop an awareness of themselves regarding their abilities and the values of cooperation and responsibility to the community in meeting basic life needs. They become one with nature.

The Advanced phase of the program continues to place youth in a camping community where everyone shares responsibility for community by living equally. Emphasis is placed on the interdependency of community members through using skills learned in the Beginning phase in a cooperative effort to sustain peaceful and productive life in a family setting. They begin to understand that they are not alone, that they do not need to fight others to become part of a group or to find peace and fulfillment of basic needs.

Participants continue individual and group counseling as new perspectives on old values and assumptions begin to become internalized. The therapeutic relationship and healing is ongoing and develops at a rate that is comfortable for the individual to begin changing some of their attitudes or to make a total shift in their paradigm.

The Ranch phase of the program emphasizes working with the family group as a unit. The student learns the value of trust and integrity, and that within the unit each person's actions affect everyone. They begin understanding that we are all interdependent.

The skills learned in the first two phases help teach the student independence and leadership, which they utilize in their scholastic venues such as GED, high school and college correspondence courses. They begin seeing the value of what higher education can bring in terms of success and reintegration into society.

Within this phase participants continue to communicate directly with their parents in a conference call designed to work on communication and integration back into their home environment. During the final two-days of Ranch, parents are given the opportunity to attend the graduation and parenting seminar, and are invited to tour the on-site facilities (Mountain Homes Ranch Webpage).

The focus of this chapter was to provide a variety of resources and programs that individuals working and interacting with juvenile and child delinquents could use to investigate options for interventions. In no way does this author endorse one program over another. Each program has some uniqueness that may make it successful with one child and unsuccessful with another. There are many factors that need to be evaluated and documented before one program is chosen over another.

Some of these programs are for individual children and youths, others for schools and school districts, and others for community. The important thing to remember is that there are options and all individuals involved with this population of troubled youth can take action and can be preventative in making sure that another youth or child at risk does not become a statistic or a fatality of our society.

Chapter 10

National Residential Programs

Life has happened and a young person is no longer able to remain with family and or in the community where their home is. What happens now? If a youth is suffering from behavioral, social, emotional, or psychological concerns there are places throughout the country that a parent can turn to.

Families of means can afford to shop around and place their child or youth in a program that hopefully meets the needs of the child. Many families are forced to go out of state to find the right fit for the youth's needs. Parents experience the loss of placing a child in a residential setting for an extended period of time. The time factor is often determined by the severity of the child or youth's needs and challenges.

Some public school districts are obliged to pay for out of district placements, which can run in the neighborhood of $70–100,000 for one single child/youth. School districts must provide the necessary programming according to the federal law IDEA. If the child/youth is identified with a specific disability according to the federal list of eligibility then services must be provided and paid for by the home school district of the student. This process is often lengthy and very detailed before a child/youth is removed from their home schools. Most districts try to accommodate this population within their own network of programs and services.

If a child/youth is unable to be provided for and educated within the system an out of district placement becomes the challenge. The goal of the collaborative team including the parents is to find a school or setting that will meet the needs of the child/youth.

CHECKLIST FOR SPECIAL EDUCATORS AND PARENTS

What does an educator and a parent look for when seeking a new residential placement for a child/youth with difficulties?

1. Accreditation: Is the school-setting recognized by legitimate educational and/or mental health agencies?
2. Population: What is the adult to child ratio?
3. Educational programming: Which curriculums are being followed and taught for the child/youth educational needs?
4. Therapeutic practices: What are the main beliefs regarding therapeutic and mental practices? Is the program based on a specific theory, ex., Glasser, Behavioral-cognitive etc?
5. Openness to visit and observe: How open is the facility in speaking about their programs, or is there an air of secrecy? Are the grounds open for inspection at any time? Are parents encouraged to come and be part of the program or therapeutic interventions? Are parents only allowed supervised visits?
6. Living conditions: Are children/youth subjugated to unhealthy or threatening practices, as in wildlife nature survival experiences where there is danger? Are housing and facilities clean and properly managed?
7. Qualified Personnel: Are the people working there qualified and licensed to practice the therapeutic or educational programming?
8. Assessment: Are children/youth assessed regularly for progress and skill acquisition? Are there reporting measures and updates given to parents or educational personnel?
9. Aversive punishment practices: Are children or youth forced to endure unprofessional or unethical disciplinary practices when not adhering to the school policy?
10. Reputation: What kind of reputation does the school or placement have? Is there available information or is there secrecy about their practices? Do state officials know about the school and what they profess to be doing? Are previous parents or students available to speak to the practices and environment?

There are many questions that a parent needs to ask that are particular to their child's needs. The list above is not exhaustive or complete, it is but a starting point to make sure that the right placement is found for the right child/youth.

A search was done of some of the more prominent programs in the USA. This list in no way endorses any of these programs or their programming. It is for information purposes only. It is highly recommended that parents, educators, or mental health professionals looking to place a troubled youth may want to begin at looking at some of these programs in much more depth.

1) Who: Diamond Ranch Academy
   Where: Utah, four separate schools in four different areas across the state. The main office is in Hurricane, Utah
   Contact Info: (435) 635.4297 Diamond Ranch Academy 1500 East 2700 South Hurricane, Utah 84737
   Program Highlights: Four separate campuses to focus on the specific needs of age groups and genders. Crystal Springs for girls ages 12–16, Whisper Creek for girls ages 16–18, Stone Ridge for boys ages 12–16 and Lava Falls for boys ages 16–18. Program has received a positive review from Dr. Taylor Hartman, who is a psychotherapist and a best-selling author.
   Cost: $5,600 a month.
   Mission: A core belief of Diamond Ranch Academy is that struggling teens have simply reversed many of life's principles of successful living by accepting society's trend to justify and minimize personal behavior. To counter this trend, we believe personal accountability and responsibility are vital principles for a foundation of successful living. It is out of this belief that an incredibly simple and effective program was created.
   Successes: An abundance of positive parent testimonials. It has an A+ rating from the Better Business Bureau. Diamond Ranch offers a guarantee. If a graduate starts to slip after they have left, Diamond Ranch will take them back at no cost to the parents. They will do this on a month-to-month basis. They have had over 550 graduates and only 34 were sent back.

2) Who: Brandon School
   Where: Natick, Massachusetts
   Contact information: 27 Winter St. Natick MA 508.655.6400 (visit the website for an extensive email list) http://www.brandonschool.org/
   Program highlights: Boys home, rapid assessment of fire-setting behaviors, intensive fire-setting treatment, sexualized behaviors program, behavioral treatment residences and transitional group home, special education day school.
   Availability: Approx.75 boys
   Mission Statement:
   -To create a diverse environment which is safe, respectful, nurturing, supportive, tolerant, and positive for all.

-To provide the highest quality residential, educational, clinical, and case management services.

-To emphasize individual growth while promoting positive social attitudes.

-To utilize the expertise and talents of all staff and foster professional growth.

-To efficiently manage program resources, while holding each other accountable for managing our own responsibilities.

-Instill a sense of pride in the Brandon community.

Goals: "The goal of Brandon's treatment program is to move boys as quickly as possible to a less restrictive school and home setting. Accordingly, the scope of our services extends not only to the boy as an individual, but also to his family. Intensive work with families is designed to successfully reunify and reintegrate boys back into their homes and communities. Brandon places significant emphasis on permanency planning. Each of our programmatic elements prepares boys to succeed alongside peers when they return to their communities."

3) Who: Germaine Lawrence

Where: Arlington, Massachusetts

Contact info: 18 Claremont Ave Arlington MA 02476, 781.648.6200

Program Highlights: Jane Addams Treatment Center: Sexual aggression and fire setting and other high-risk behaviors

Cynthia Browning Treatment Center: STARR and CBAT short term assessment and stabilization.

ACT Group Home: Girls who have been, or are at risk for being, commercially sexually exploited.

Saul M. Hirschberg Treatment Center: Eating disorders and other medically compromised conditions.

Katharine E. Merck Treatment Center: Individualized treatment for high-risk behaviors.

Tubman Treatment Residence (BTR and Group Home): Therapeutic treatment with a community school component.

Availability: can serve almost 100 girls 7–12 months

Mission Statement:

"The mission of Germaine Lawrence is to provide adolescent girls the highest quality residential treatment services with the goal of strengthening their relationships with their families and preparing them for productive, independent lives. Further, it is the mission to design, implement, and disseminate treatment approaches that define new standards of excellence in the field, and through this leadership to improve the quality of care available to troubled adolescent girls."

Successes:

"In 2008, 58 girls were discharged from Germaine Lawrence's long term programs, including Addams, Hirschberg, Snowden and Merck. 72% successfully completed program goals and had planned discharges to their families or a less-restrictive level of care; 17% had unplanned discharges due to running, hospitalization, or transfer to another residential facility; and 10% were withdrawn by their parents or themselves (for those over 18) without meeting program goals. Four girls (7%) stayed for less than one month. For most girls (93%), the average length of stay was 14.2 months. Age upon admission ranged from 12 to 19, with an average age of 16.

Of the 72% of girls who had planned discharges, 64% were discharged to parents/families, 5% to foster families, and 31% to less-restrictive levels of care (Behavior Treatment Residential and Group Homes). At the follow-up interview three months after discharge, only four girls (9%) had moved to a more restrictive setting. All of the other girls (91%) were either living at the same place to which they were discharged or at a similar or lower level of care.

With regard to education, for all girls with planned discharges, 17% (7 girls) had graduated from high school. Of these seven, two girls were attending community college and four girls had plans to attend. The remaining 83% of girls (35) who had planned discharges did not yet have their high school diplomas. 94% of these girls (33) were enrolled in school.

As for behavior, 91% of all girls with planned discharges had no arrests or legal detentions since discharge, and 85% had no hospitalizations since discharge."

4) Who: Robert F. Kennedy Children's Action Corps
Where: Throughout Massachusetts
Contact Info: Robert F. Kennedy Children's Action Corps 11 Beacon street suite 200 Boston MA, 02108 617.227.4183 or 877.735.3500
Program Highlights:
Availability: Cape Cod 12 beds 45 days
Lancaster- over 50 beds stay is 1 month to 1 year
South Hadley- 16 girls
Springfield- 120 boys, white street group home- 12 beds
Westborough- Robert F. Kennedy school- 20 boys, Fay A. Rotenberg School-15 girls
Mission statement:
RFK Children's Action Corps is dedicated to improving the lives of children and families throughout Massachusetts, and to making a lasting

contribution to society as a whole. Our mission is guided by our core values and beliefs.

We believe in the legacy of Robert F. Kennedy—that society has a responsibility to the poor and disadvantaged.

In respecting the dignity and individuality of every human being.

That all children have the right to grow up in a safe and nurturing environment.

That every person has the right to reach his or her full potential.

Goal: That every child live as we would want our own children to live.

Success: While young people are in care, they demonstrate significant improvement in their ability to interact with others in healthy ways and in their personal health and hygiene. They also show dramatic improvement in their school performance, often improving by several grades in reading and math in their first few months. What's more, at least one adolescent in care receives his or her GED every year.

Due to the confidential nature of the work, the school is not permitted to follow the progress of young people after they leave care. However, many of those who have been through our programs call to speak to staff members who've helped them and in that way learn of the role played in their success. Some of these youths have graduated from college and even received master's degrees. They often tell that we provided the first environment where they felt happy, healthy, safe, and secure. http://www.rfkchildren.org/uploads/press/Its%20work%20staying%20out%20of%20trouble.pdf http://www.rfkchildren.org//index.php?page=our-stories

5) Who: Willow Springs Center

Where: Reno, Nevada

Contact Info: Willow Springs Center, 690 Edison Way Reno, NV 89502 775.858.3303

Program Highlights: Locked residential facility. Has a pediatric program for 5–12 year olds. Uses cognitive behavioral therapy. Offers a survivors group. Has a 20 bed Dialectical Behavior Therapy program designed to treat people with borderline personality disorder. Uses the Matrix Model of Relapse Prevention which incorporates a 12-step program. Offers a ropes course as well.

Cost: $54,960.60 per year

Availability: 116- bed facility

Mission: At Willow Springs, we are compassionate, committed and caring people, dedicated to inspire hope, as well as the ability to achieve and celebrate success through the power of relationships developed with children, families, and the communities we support.

Willow Springs promotes clinical excellence, an environment of collaboration and trust while maintaining fiscal responsibility and integrity for patients, customers and the communities we serve. Successes: http://willowspringscenter.com/index.php?p=testimonials

Over 10 different testimonials from students that attended

6) Who: Eagle Ranch Academy

Where: St. George, Utah

Contact Info: 115 W 1470 S St. George UT 84770 888.698.7095

Program Highlights: Value based behavior change creating long term results by teaching real life values

Life Skills Coaching Program- only found at ERA

Small staff to student ratio

Recreational, social and cultural activities such as camping, BBQ's, kayaking, rafting, trips to Zion Park, Grand Canyon, Snow Canyon, etc.

Cost: $7500 a month

Availability: 48 students at a time

Mission/Philosophy: Eagle Ranch Academy is dedicated to making a difference in the lives of troubled teens. Our focus is on troubled teens struggling with issues, but with special talents—academic, athletic, leadership, performing arts, or some other special ability. We believe these young people will someday make significant contributions to themselves, their families, and to OUR Communities. All they need is to get back on track with their lives, and once again begin to enjoy their youth with their families and friends, and have the opportunity to maximize their special talents.

7) Who: Stetson School for Boys

Where: Barre, Massachusetts

Contact Info: Kathy O'Connor, Admissions CoordinatorStetson School, Inc. 455 South

Street P.O. Box 309 Barre, MA 01005–0309 phone 978.355.4541

Program Highlights: Pioneer in sex abuser specific services for children and youth, over 40 years as a treatment center for at-risk youth. Has a special 40 week core program that specializes in the treatment of children and youth with Sexual Behavior Problems.

Program Highlights: Pioneer in sex abuser specific services for children and youth

Over 40 years as a treatment center for youth at risk

Clinician/Student ratio 1:8

Provide admission interview in student's home state

Stetson will provide transportation on admission day if it is within 250 miles.

Availability: 120 beds average stay 18 mos.

Mission: Stetson School provides healing and learning opportunities in a safe and nurturing environment to help children, adolescents, and young adults with special needs to reach their full potential. Stetson School maintains the belief that every child can succeed. We believe that every child deserves the opportunity to become a confident, capable adult, and a productive member of the community.

Our philosophy encourages moral development, an inner sense of compassion, and personal and social responsibility. Such growth and development begins in a safe environment in which the child's life experience has positive meaning and purpose, and where nonviolence and treating others with dignity and respect are primary values.

Successes: "Stetson School has a documented record of discharging youth to lower levels of care. For the period July 1 to December 31, 2005, 84% of Stetson School youth were discharged to lower levels of care including 31% discharged home, 15% to a foster home, 50% to a community group home, and 4% to independent living programs. Treatment teams strive toward the shortest duration of care in a restrictive environment that makes sense for the youth's needs."

8) Who: Meridell Achievement Center
   Where: Liberty Hill, Texas
   Contact Info: Meridell Achievement Center PO Box 87 Liberty Hill, Texas 78642 (512) 528–2100
   Cost: $450–480 a day depending on the program.
   Program Highlights: Has a program for just about every type of struggling child or adolescent, is part of Universal Health Services.
   Availability: 134 beds
   Mission: "We are committed to providing the highest quality of care in an atmosphere that nurtures healing and growth."
   Goal: "The goal of Meridell is to provide the highest quality of care in a nurturing and healing manner."

9) Who: Benchmark Behavioral Health Systems
   Where: Woods Cross, Utah
   Contact Info: Benchmark Behavioral Health Systems 592 West 1350 South, Woods
   Cross, Utah 04087
   Program Highlights: Uses Family Focused Programming, also uses Recreation Therapy, has several different programs for Juvenile and adolescent sex offenders as well as oppositional youth. Has a program for sex offenders who were unsuccessful in other programs.
   Availability: 68 beds, average stay, 12–18 months.

Mission: Located on the Wasatch Front, high in the Rocky Mountains, Benchmark Hospital provides a state of the art high security facility in a beautiful majestic setting. Benchmark's combined emphasis on behavioral and psycho-educational intervention results in a program that is effective, revolutionary, and successful. Through the wide range of program components and intensive treatment, our chief concern is the youth. We are committed to developing youth who can return to their families and into society able to lead normal, productive lives.

10) Who: New Haven Residential Treatment Center

Where: Spanish Fork, Utah

Contact Info: New Haven 2172 E 7200 S. Spanish Fork, UT 84660 888.877.3044 admissions@newhavenrtc.com

Program Highlights: Therapeutic Boarding school for girls. Uses the family works approach. Member of Inner Change, Accredited by the Joint Commission, member of NATSAP (National Association of Therapeutic Schools and Programs, Certified in the Equine Assisted Growth and learning Association, is on the US' Student and Exchange Visitor Program (meaning they have clearance to accept immigrant students and it is a member of the Better Business Bureau.

Cost: Enrollment fee of $1,500. $475.00 per day

Availability: Rolling applications, average stay 10–12 months. Approx. 16 students at a time

Goals: Our goal is for the students to return home and to their families. Our most recent outcome study shows that 90% of students return home! Others may choose to go to boarding school, to college, or other treatment, if necessary.

11) Who: Oxbow Academy

Where: Wales, Utah

Contact Info: 95 North State HC Box 4254 Wales, UT 84667 435.436.9460

Program Highlights: They are holistic based not shame based. Students use the Good Lives Model to discover the skills they possess before they began participating in inappropriate sexual activity. Member of the Association for the Treatment for Sexual Abusers. Member of the Utah Network on Juveniles Offending Sexually. 4 Phases of treatment that focus on specific areas of need. Each student develops their own mission statement and is required to recite it to the group twice a day.

Availability: 24 students at a time, lasting approx. 9 months

Mission: We are engaged in and dedicated to helping out students and their families identify and disrupt negative behavioral patterns while enhancing, supporting, developing and internalizing positive living patterns and principles. We accomplish this by demonstrating a passionate commitment to honesty, integrity, understanding, love, compassion, patience and personal accountability to the treatment process.

Successes: Studies show if you intervene at an early age, with someone who has a sexual problem success is 80–90% more likely than if you wait until they are adults.

"Juveniles are much more amenable to treatment," Brooks notes. He says statistics show an 80–90% success rate. With adults the outlook is not nearly so positive. "The numbers are almost inverted for adults" (http://oxbowacademy.net/archives/1992).

12) Who: Pine Haven

Where: Allenstown, New Hampshire

Contact Info: 133 River Rd. PO Box 162 Allenstown, NH 03275 603.485.7142 phbc@comcast.net

Program Highlights: Only school in NH that has a fire program.

Availability: 20 students at a time

Mission: Pine Haven is committed to providing children with positive experiences and success oriented programs. The process is to identify appropriate behaviors: catching the child doing right. The ultimate goal is to have the youngster return to his family, school and community. When reunification is not the plan, Pine Haven is committed to promoting the optimal possible level of involvement between the child and his family. Pine Haven honors the dignity, resources and strengths of families and is dedicated to involving them in all major decisions affecting their children.

13) Who: Heartland Behavioral Health Services

Where: Nevada, Missouri

Contact Info: 2010 Heartland Behavioral Services • 1500 West Ashland Street, Nevada, MO 64772 • (800) 654–9605

Program Highlights: Equestrian Program, ropes course, tennis courts, accredited by the Joint Commission, offers a sexually abusive youth program

Mission: The mission of Heartland is to provide programs and services that will improve the overall health and well-being of children and their families. We achieve this by providing exceptional care through a talented team of health professionals. Our clinical team works diligently to build on the strengths of the child and to provide them with the support they need to mend their emotional wounds.

Goals: Our goal is to positively impact the life of a child. We want to provide special opportunities for our children to grow, learn, and return to their communities.

14) Who: Eckerd Youth Academy
Where: Florida and Georgia
Contact Info: Eckerd Youth Alternatives, Inc.100 Starcrest DriveClearwater, FL 33765Tel. 727–461–2990
Program Highlights: Won 2010 non-profit of the year sponsored by the Tampa Bay Business Journal, Florida's first private outdoor therapeutic program for troubled teens. Features -Positive Peer Culture with non-punitive discipline, Individualized treatment and academic plans, Psychiatrist for medication management, Weekly individual, group and family counseling, Weekly Art Therapy Blue Ridge campus, Weekly Substance Abuse Group, Aftercare and follow-up, Experiential trips—museums, nature hikes, mountain biking and canoe trips
Availability: 60 beds
Mission: Develop and share programs that promote the well-being of children and serve at-risk youth and their families.
Successes: "A large majority of youth in our programs graduate with considerable gains in self-concept and confidence. More than 80% make significant educational gains in reading and math (more than 2 years gain on average). These are tremendous achievements for youths who were previously spiraling downward."

15) Who: Moonridge Academy
Where:Murray, Utah
Contact Info: Moonridge AcademyPO Box 575780, Murray UT 84157
Telephone: 435–559–2823 Email: info@teen-depression.org
Program Highlights: Age appropriate treatment, i.e. keeping the older girls and younger girls separated. Play time is built into schedule. Horseback riding.
Availability: 16 girls at a time
Mission: "The core philosophy of both Moonridge Academy . . . is that there is greatness within each of us. We all have a special place where courage, love, hope, honor, and dreams live, where strength and ability lay waiting to be used. This is the 'real' us."
Successes: more than 10 testimonials of student successes on the webpage.
(See also Kolob Canyon Residential Treatment Center)

16) Who: Perkins- The Premier Special Education Facility
Where: Lancaster, Massachusetts
Contact Info: 971 Main Street, Lancaster, MA 01523 978.365.7376
www.perkinsprograms.org
Program Highlights: Therapeutic Horsemanship Program, Care and Nurturing Small Animal Program, High Five (Ropes) Outdoor Adventure Program, Mini-bike Program

Swimming, Basketball, Soccer, Soft Ball, Hobby Groups, Culinary Cooking, Dances and Socials, Cultural Events and Trips.

"Few child welfare agencies can boast the solid program, professional staff, spacious campus and state of the art facilities (one school superintendent described it as "to die for") that Perkins possesses. We pride ourselves in providing the best care with commitment, dedication and compassion for kids who often have significant challenges to surmount."

Mission: "Our mission is to continue a tradition of leadership and innovation in providing a range of educational programs and human services to meet family and community needs and enhance human development. We have been doing this work longer than most others and we believe we do it better."

Successes: In 2010 eight students graduated their senior year. They received formal recognized diplomas.

17) Who: Newport Academy

Where: Newport Beach, California

Contact Info: 877–628–3367

Program highlights: Provides adolescents with a minimum of 36 hours of therapy per week, uses gender specific treatment, which is "recognized by the American Medical Association as a key element of effective adolescent treatment."

Cost: Approximately $1,000 dollars a day.

Availability: 12 students at a time, 6 boys and 6 girls.

Mission: "Newport Academy is dedicated to providing comprehensive, gender-specific, integrated treatment programs for adolescent males and females in an environment of caring and compassion by which teens and their families may recover from the destructive effects of substance abuse and related behavioral health issues." Has an active alumni program, uses equine therapy.

18) Who: Catherine Freer Wilderness Therapy Programs

Where: Albany, Oregon

Contact Info: Catherine Freer PO Box 1064 Albany, OR 97321 800.390.3983

Cost: $1,000 equipment fee $150 processing fee, a $2,500 deposit and $485 a day tuition

Program Highlights: "ours is the only therapeutic wilderness program in the country where a master's level therapist, with drug and alcohol counseling experience, is a member of the staff team that resides in the field with the adolescents. This creates an unmatched therapeutic relationship resulting in remarkable outcomes for children."

Mission: In pristine wilderness areas, where eagles soar and deer and elk roam, is where we'll help your child discover their strengths, confront their weaknesses, and experience success. With no cell phones to distract them nor pressures from peers, school or home, your child will begin to "slow down" and address the issues that are causing them to struggle.

Successes: Catherine Freer boasts that it is one of the "best researched adolescent programs in the US."

Two to three years later 83% of graduates are "doing better."

In one study they found that regular marijuana use went from 44% before treatment to 3% six months after treatment.

For more info visit http://www.cfreer.com/outcome-research/index.php

19) Who: Woodlands Spring Lodge

Where: Saint James, Missouri

Contact Info: PO Box 189 Saint James, Missouri 65559 573.265.3251 www.woodlandsprings.org

Mission/Philosophy: The treatment philosophy at Woodland Spring Lodge is centered on the premise that children who are experiencing emotional or behavioral problems have experienced interruptions in the normal development of the attachment process. We believe that normal attachment is based on three levels of trust: trust of care, trust of control and trust of self. Developing the ability to bond is a basic building block of human relationships and is essential to friendship, marriage, parenting, work relationships, and a meaningful, moral participation in society (Ray Curtis, Evergreen Colorado).

At Woodland Spring Lodge the focus of our treatment is to have children re-learn the normal attachment stages in order to develop a healthy and appropriate adult-child bond.

Most of our children suffer from maladaptive child-adult relationships. The emphasis of our program is to uncover the causes of these incongruent relationships and to develop positive attitudes toward building trusting and respectful relationships. The child is taught to understand and master their maladaptive behaviors while living in our residential setting. Until a child is able to understand the reasons for their defiant reaction to healthy adult-child relationships and expectations, they will continue to react to structure with defiant behaviors.

At Woodland Spring Lodge we create a "living environment" based on trust, providing children the experiences to develop and maintain positive and meaningful relationships. The basis for developing and fostering age-appropriate developmental attachment is the one-on-one interaction between child and staff that is created in the living environment of Woodland Spring Lodge.

20) Who: Turnabout Stillwater Academy
Where: South Jordan, Utah
Contact Info: Turnabout Stillwater Academy 11175 South Redwood Rd
South Jordan, Utah 84095 866–359–4600 (toll free) 801–484–9911ad-
missions@turnaboutteens.org
Cost: $4,850 a month, plus fees $51,000 a year.
Program Highlights: Some activities students participate in- annual
cattle drive, hiking backpacking, trail rides, appropriate concerts. They
use video conferencing, a private login account so that parents can see
their child's progress, aftercare, equine therapy, and special housing that
models a home-like setting.
Availability: rolling admissions
Mission: It is the mission of Stillwater Academy to Support the emotional growth of students, Build confidence in their ability to meet academic standards and goals, and Inspire a love of learning.
Turnabout Stillwater Academy believes that student learning is the
chief priority of school—students learn in different ways and should
be provided with a variety of instructional approaches to support their
learning.–Each student is a valued individual with unique physical,
social, emotional and intellectual needs. Exceptional students (special
education, limited English proficiency, talented and gifted, etc.) require
special services and resources.
Goals: Help youth rediscover the talented, capable, and worthwhile
individuals they are -Help youth reestablish healthy, positive relationships with their families. Provide a safe and supportive environment that
encourages youth to identify the underlying issues driving their negative
and self-destructive behaviors -Help youth gain the courage to change
and develop healthy, positive coping skills. Support youth through the
unknown and sometimes frightening process of change Teach youth
to support each other and learn the value of true, healthy friendships.
Maintain a positive peer culture based on love and support. Teach parents in crisis the skills they need to help themselves and their families.
Help parents become positive, powerful, and insightful. Assist parents
in improving their own personal relationships. Help parents find within
themselves the power to change. Support and encourage parents through
this process of personal growth and change, which is vital for the program to have lasting and valuable effect. Foster support amongst youth,
parents, and the community. Teach youth and parents to give back and
support the program
Alternative Programs

21) Who: SUWS

Strategy: "We believe that our combination of wilderness environment and experiential learning activities create the ideal therapeutic milieu in which to help students recognize and build upon their own sense of self-worth as they learn the value of helping others."

They use the "search and rescue" metaphor to help students address their issues.

Mission/Goals:

SUWS is designed to meet the needs of students who are struggling to overcome the internal conflicts and external obstacles that have hampered their ability to achieve their greatest potential.

We embrace CRC's five core values:

Respect—for our patients, our employees, and our community

Integrity—in our dealings with all those whose lives we touch

Accountability—to our patients and their families, and to our colleagues

Responsibility—for the decisions we make and the actions we take

Excellence—in every task we perform

Brief Overview: SUWS is a wilderness therapy program located in Shoshone, Idaho. They address teens struggling with many issues. Angry, defiant, rebellious, impulsive teens using drugs and alcohol and teen runaways, to name a few. Students may also be experiencing mood disorders, low self-esteem and ADHD.

SUWS uses a three phase approach

Phase 1: Individual- addresses student's individual needs and emphasizes accountability and personal responsibility. Students spend time hiking and camping with their group, but they are primarily alone with their thoughts.

Phase 2: Family- students become more integrated into the group. They are given tasks and responsibilities that will affect both themselves and the group.

Phase 3: Community- In this phase the lessons from the other phases become integrated and the student demonstrates the ability to contribute to the greater community. Ask themselves reflective questions like "How are we going to act in a way that helps and serves others?"

The lessons they learn- self-confidence, maturity, and many others- they can take with them and apply them to any situation they may face in life.

22) Who: Aspen Ranch

Strategy: Aspen Ranch uses a combination of living in a therapeutic environment, attending an individually paced school designed for success, participating in individual and group therapy, and involvement in a life-changing Equine Program. This allows Aspen Ranch students to experience success and rediscover a sense of mastery and self-worth.

Mission/Goals: Aspen Ranch, an environment where adolescents can develop, practice and improve healthy interdependence, social accountability, responsibility and self-mastery through principle based decision making, value congruent behavior, and honest achievement in a traditional ranch setting.

Brief Overview: Aspen Ranch is located in Loa, Utah. They use a variety of therapeutic methods including equine therapy to help the students realize their potential and begin to work toward changing. The students are split by gender. In the morning the girls focus on experiential activities such as the equine therapy, while the boys are in school. In the afternoon they switch. Throughout the week the students are involved in other things like peer meeting and evening meetings. And even their schoolwork is based around discussing prevention and their moods and so on.

Aspen Ranch works through a level system and only through honesty and achievement can the students work their way through the levels.

23) Who: Wilderness Treatment Center—A boys only substance abuse treatment center, located in Marion, Montana.

Strategy: Rugged challenging activities such as backpacking, cross country skiing, rappelling, ranch work, and a wilderness expedition, offer adventure and in a disciplined setting that leads to effective change for these young men & male teens.

Mission/Goals: Our treatment center's primary goal is to introduce male teens & young adult males to a new way of life free from drugs and alcohol with increased self-esteem and a feeling of empowerment.

Brief Overview: Wilderness Treatment Center is a 60 day inpatient chemical dependency addiction treatment facility for teens / young men between the ages of 14 and 24. We combine a conventional 30 day inpatient stay with a 16–21 day wilderness adventure expedition. As always, each of the expeditions is staffed by one of the addiction counselors and a wilderness instructor for the duration of the trip. The two components and length of stay allow Wilderness Treatment Center graduates to be further in the addiction recovery process than those leaving other programs. http://www.wilderness-therapy-program.com/

24) Wilderness Quest, Utah

Strategy: Through a combination of intensive wilderness living and strongly facilitated 12-step model self-discovery, students achieve changes in substance use/abuse, personal responsibility, accountability, maturity and behavior.

Mission/Goals: Bringing families back together

Brief Overview: Wilderness Quest uses the wilderness therapy model to challenge the students. Students need to be responsible for gathering fire wood and building a shelter, if they do not take care of themselves there is no one to blame but themselves.

Wilderness Quest students are put in difficult circumstances where their perception of being at risk is heightened (i.e. independent night hike, weather challenges, solo, climbing and rappelling). They discover they are responsible for and capable of; building shelters, gathering wood, cooking food over a fire made without matches, carving spoons, and hiking in heat, cold, rain or snow to reach a destination.

Staff is with the students 24 hours a day.

Wilderness Quest uses the 12-step treatment program and also focuses on family relationships.

25) Montcalm Schools, Outside in Program

Strategy: Montcalm Schools' "Outside In" program is helping meet the social, emotional, behavioral and educational needs of this group of children through its strength-based, youth empowerment model.

Mission/Goals: There's no such thing as a bad kid.

Brief Overview: Outside in helps children with PDD to meet the social, emotional, behavioral and educational needs by using a strength-based, youth empowerment model. Outside in focuses on students inner strengths and talents by creating an environment filled with consistency, trust and patience.

Residential school for youths age 12–21

Year round schooling with rolling admissions

A positive peer culture environment where students can practice and learn from one another

A strength based treatment philosophy that builds self-esteem.

In conclusion, this list of programs is but a small sample of what is available in the USA, as part of alternative program and programming. Each one of these programs highlights a specific area that they have decided to specialize in. The children and youth who need these specialized programs are often very damaged children who will not be successful in a public school. Their needs are so great that only in receiving these specialized services can they hope to graduate from high school, to learn coping skills, to be able to interact socially and above all to find a path that they can navigate through life.

Specialized schools and treatment facilities are often seen as last resorts for many kids. The important thing to remember is that the children and youth who need these services or sites do so if they are going to have the slightest chance at some sort of success in life. Without these places and programs many youths will be a death statistic because of the violence that permeates their lives. We need to act responsibly to make sure that all children and youth who need this extra help get it. It is our duty as educators and professionals to help parents find what will serve the needs of their child best. After all, is that not why we are in the business of helping and educating?

Epilogue

Children in Crisis: an eye-catching phrase, but one loaded with much pain and misery. Life in 2011 has become a burden for so many. If we look back over history, the youngest members of societies have always been the most vulnerable and expendable. They are born into poverty, abuse, violence, and at times inhospitable conditions; some survive, and others perish early.

What are the factors that seem to be present in those children who are able to navigate through adolescence and move into adulthood with a skill set that allows them to be successful? This skill set seems to be based on resilience and an ability to adapt. The adaptation of a species allows for its survival. Have we created a whole generation of children and youth who have adapted to the dysfunction of life in the twenty-first century? Absolutely!

It is a well-known fact that one's early years' experiences have a major impact in the formation of personality, cognitive and social emotional growth, and development. The information in this book identified many factors that are lurking in the home, school, and community that will impair or damage the appropriate development in these areas. We recognize them, yet we continue to encourage their development and maintain the status quo in many instances.

When investigating the causes of dysfunction, we see the root as being a lack of the skills necessary to be successful in life. If we look at the skill set of children in crisis, they are remarkable in that their skill sets involving manipulation, power and control, dishonesty, lying, and cheating are all very well-defined and honed to a level of perfection that enables their survival. We, as a mainstream society, see these behaviors as a problem as they cost the tax payers huge amounts of money to clean up, jail, or provide services to enable these youths to be functioning members of society. We have not been very successful in these areas, as the numbers of youths in trouble keeps growing every year.

Is the answer more services and money to the service providers? Money is definitely a factor that provides help to families and youth who are struggling, but at what point should money be given? The budgets for many social services and juvenile justice services are phenomenal, yet youth crime is still on the rise in certain parts of the United States. We see social service departments unable to find foster care and housing for children removed from their homes due to parental neglect and abuse. Our juvenile justice detention centers do not have enough beds to house all the young criminals who are involved in some sort of violence. At what point can American society no longer support the detention of troubled youth?

The capacity to support adolescent juvenile delinquents, runaways, drug addicts, prostitutes and petty criminals is at a breaking point in many communities. It is imperative that the individuals involved in education, politics, and law enforcement become more proactive in teaching skills to young children and youth, so that they may become law-abiding citizens as well as productive members of society. Education and the teaching of new skill sets is the answer.

Early intervention is the key to understanding and supporting children and youth with new skills that will make them successful. There is so much disparity in economics that many of the causes of the behavior or acting out is rooted deep in this desire to be able to have all the basics of life, but also to be given the benefits that money seems to provide. Children and youth are not able to see that material things need to be earned, not just taken. If a child does not have the skills to get these desired objects, such as education or supportive training, they will not be able to achieve what they so desire. A desire creates the pathway to the behaviors. If one is able to gain something through one's efforts and time, and is successful, that individual will continue to work at achieving at a higher level. Failure to do so will only create other coping skills that are often based in violence and crime.

What is the responsibility of the school system? Schools are provided as a means to educate the masses in ways that will enable the student to become self-reliant, more intelligent in their understanding of certain concepts, and will provide the pathway to success, financially through a college education, and hopefully a fulfilling career. What about the youths who do not have the opportunity, or the intellectual capacity to achieve a college education or a prosperous career? Are they given the crumbs? What about their development and financial success? We as a society need to begin changing the disparity that exists within our society. There will always be richer people, but why are there poor people? Can we not be creative in giving every woman, man, and child a decent standard of life where they are able to survive beyond day-to-day existence?

As you read the different chapters, it was my hope that you were able to get a comprehensive portrait of the issue, step away with a new understanding and awareness, but to really take it to the next step and ask what is it that I can do to make this situation better. How can I take the knowledge gained and become a change agent when working with children and youth in crisis? What are the actions and outcomes that I can effect in my community or in my school?

The goal in writing this book was to change perspectives and build awareness of problems that are often in the headlines, but are often ignored unless it has directly affected the individual through a personal experience or trauma. It sometimes is much easier to walk around, over, or above a problem and not pay attention but how long can we do this? As the many statistics in this book have highlighted, we can no longer be uninvolved; we need to rally and become involved. We cannot be bystanders, yet so many of us are. We take refuge in our locked homes, watch the 6 pm news, say oh, my god frequently, turn the television off and go on our merry way.

We spend billions of dollars on war activities in destinations around the world, yet we have a war here in America. There is a whole generation of youth who are disenfranchised and lost. They wander the streets of America in search of something. That something is often unattainable and undefined. We invest money and time into programs and resources, yet we never really deal with the root cause of the behavior. America is very good at putting on Band-Aids, but never looks for the cure.

There are millions of youth in America that are throw-away human beings. They are seen as a liability to the country and treated as such. These youths are an eyesore to the American persona worldwide. This shows America's vulnerability, but also its failure at meeting the needs of many of its citizens. The all-powerful American educational system is no longer a front runner worldwide. We have been decreasing in effectiveness year after year, yet we do nothing to change an antiquated system that is not meeting the needs of a large portion of American youths. The at-risk population is growing by leaps and bounds and fewer youths are making it to college, thus creating a wider divide between the socioeconomic groups within American society.

The answer is not to throw money at families and communities, but to educate in a way that individuals have the opportunity to gain skills that will enable them to achieve their goals and desires. Not everyone wants to be an astronaut, a lawyer, a teacher, or a doctor, but people should be given the opportunity to gain skills in order to have a quality life. People need to be given support when overwhelmed with life and parenthood so as to be able to nurture and take care of their children. Should people have a license to have a child? Should children only be produced by the rich, smartest, and the best only?

It would be argued by those who are the richest, smartest, and most successful that all the ills of American society would be cured if certain people would not be allowed to reproduce. Who or what should have that kind of power to decide? Governments? Doctors? Scientists?

This book is a compilation of many different factors that create children in crisis but it is also a book of hope. The hope being that the reader will become an advocate for change. That instead of moving by, you will stop, help in any way you can, and make a difference in a child's or youth's life. The act of kindness, the willingness to listen, the openness to support, the lack of judgment and criticism, being genuine, and being a good person will have more of an impact than anything that money can buy.

It begins with you saying no to the status quo and becoming an agent of change. It begins with one step at a time. It begins with you. You have the power. Use it for the good of all children and youth worldwide.

May life give you the ability to help others in a way that you change them forever!

Marcel Lebrun

References

AACAP (2002, November). "Children and TV Violence." Retrieved September 12, 2010. www.aacap.org/cs/root/facts_for_families/children_and_tv_violence.

"Abused, Abandoned Juveniles Get Schooled for Adult Life," *San Diego Daily Transcript* (October 17, 1996).

Action Planning Checklist Prevention. Department of Education. www.peace.ca/actionpreven.htm, Retrieved August 5, 2010.

"Adoption Learning Partners: From Foster Family to Forever Family." Retrieved October 7, 2010. www.adoptionlearningpartners.org/foster_to_forever.cfm.

AFCARS Report (2010). U.S. Department of Health and Human Services, Administration for Children and Families, Administration on Children, Youth and Families, Children's Bureau. www.acf.hhs.gov/programs/cb.

American Academy of Child and Adolescent Psychiatry. "Children and Guns." Retrieved August 3, 2010. www.aacap.org/cs/root/policy_statements/children_and_guns.

Annie E. Casey Foundation. "Juvenile detention initiative core standards." Retrieved October 3, 2010. www.aecf.org/MajorInitiatives/JuvenileDetentionAlternativesInitiative/ CoreStrategies.aspx.

Author's analysis of OJJDP's Census of Juveniles in Residential Placement 1997, 1999, 2001, 2003, and 2006 [machine-readable data files].

Azar, B. (1995, November). "Foster Care Has Bleak History." Apa Monitor.

Bayles, F. and Cohen S., "Chaos Often the Only Parent for Abused or Neglected Children," (AP) *Los Angeles Times* (April 30, 1995).

BBC News Report (2007). Youth and Crimes Report. Retrieved November 21, 2010. news.bbc.co.uk/2/hi/6974587.stm.

BBC, World Service. (2009, November 9). "When children kill children." Available from www.bbc.co.uk/worldservice/people/highlights/001109_child.shtml.

Bender, K., et al. (2007, February). "Capacity for survival: Exploring strengths of homeless street youth." Child and Youth Care Forum, 36(1), 25–42.

Berezina, E. (2003). "Street Children." Youth Advocate Program International Resource Paper. Available from www.yapi.org/rpstreetchildren.pdf.

BJS Special Report. "Weapon use and violent crime" (NCJ 194820). www.usdoj.gov, select BJS. puborder.ncjrs.org.

Bookman, S. (2010, October 11). "5 SI Teens Arrested on Hate Crime Charges." Retrieved December 12, 2010. abclocal.go.com/wabc/story?section=news/ localandid=7718678.

Booth, C. (2002). Institute for Family Development. Available from www.strengthen-ingfamilies.org/html/programs_1999/23_HOMEBUILDERS.html.

Brezina. T., Wright, J. D. "Going armed in the school zone." Forum for Applied Research and Public Policy, 15, (4), 82–87, 2000.

Brooks, R.A., et. al. (2004, November). The system-of-care for homeless youth: perceptions of service providers. Evaluation and Program Planning, 27(4), 443–451.

Burn Institute. (n.d.). Retrieved August 8, 2010, from www.burninstitute.org/index.php.

Bynum, J. E., and Thompson, W. E. (1996). *Juvenile delinquency: A sociological approach*, 3d ed. Needham Heights, MA: Allyn and Bacon.

Campbell, Duncan (2003). "Murdered with impunity, the street children who live and die like vermin." Retrieved from www.informationclearinghouse.info/article3573.htm.

Center for Family Development (2007). "An Overview of Reactive Attachment Disorder for Teachers." Retrieved July 18, 2010. www.center4familydevelop.com/ helpteachrad.htm.

Centers for Disease Control and Prevention. Web-based Injury Statistics Query and Reporting System (WISQARS) [Online].(2009) National Center for Injury Prevention and Control, Centers for Disease Control and Prevention (producer). Available from: www.cdc.gov/injury/wisqars/index.html. [Accessed 2010 July 07.]

Centers for Disease Control and Prevention (b). Youth risk behavioral surveillance— United States, 2009. MMWR 2010;59 (No. SS–5).

Centers for Disease Control and Prevention (a).Web-based Injury Statistics Query and Reporting System (WISQARS) [Online].(2007). National Center for Injury Prevention and Control, Centers for Disease Control and Prevention (producer). [2010 Jun 14] Available from URL: www.cdc.gov/injury.

Child Defense Fund (2009, September 16). "Protect Children Not Guns." Available from www.childrensdefense.org/child-research-data-publications/data/protect-children-not-guns-report-2009.html.

Children's Mental Health Disorder Fact Sheet for the Classroom1. Reactive Attachment Disorder (RAD). Retrieved July 18, 2010. www.ksde.org/KS_SAFE_SCHOOLS_ RESOURCE _CENTER/RAD.pdfwww.joellebelmonte.com/.

Consortium to Prevent School violence, Bullying Prevention Fact Sheet. Retrieved July 29, 2010. www.preventschoolviolence.org/resources.html.

"Cutting statistics and self-injury treatment." Retrieved July 3, 2010. www.teenhelp. com/teen-health/cutting-stats-treatment.html.

Demb J. M. (1991). "Reported Hyperphagia in Foster Children." Child Abuse Neglect, 15 (1–2), 77–88.

Department of Health and Human Services (DHHS). Youth violence: a report of the Surgeon General [online]; 2001. Available from: www.surgeongeneral.gov/library/ youthviolence/toc.html.

Department of Health and Human Services (DHHS). Youth violence: a report of the Surgeon General [online]; 2001. www.surgeongeneral.gov/library/youthviolence/toc.html.

Dorn, M. and C (2006). "Seven signs a weapon is being concealed." Campus Safety Magazine July/August 2006.

Dubner, A. E., and Motta, R. W. (1999, June). "Sexually and Physically Abused Foster Care Children and Posttraumatic Stress Disorder." J Consult Clinical Psychology (3), 367–73.

Focus Adolescence Services (2008).Warning Signs. Retrieved on July 3, 2010. www.focusas.com/SubstanceAbuse-WarningSigns.html.

Foster Care by ABD Adoptions.com. Retrieved September 12, 2010. www.abcadoptions.com/foster.htm.

Gilmour J., Skuse, D., and Pembrey, M. (2001, August). "Hyperphagic short stature and Prader—Willi syndrome: A comparison of behavioural phenotypes, genotypes and indices of stress." Br J Psychiatry, 179, 129–37.

Greenberg, M. (1999). "Attachment and psychopathology in childhood." In J. Cassidy and P. Shaver (Eds.). *Handbook of Attachment.*. New York: Guilford Press, 469–496.

Greenwood, P. (2008). "Prevention and Intervention Programs for Juvenile Offenders." *The Future of Children* 18, 2, 185–210. Princeton: Princeton University Press.

Hadfield, S.C., and Preece, P.M. (2008, November). "Obesity in looked after children: is foster care protective from the dangers of obesity?" Child Care Health Dev., 34(6), 710–12.

Hawkins, D., Catalano, R. (2002). "Preparing for the drug free years." www.strengtheningfamilies.org/html/programs_1999/05_PDFY.html.

Herrenkohl, T. I., Hawkins, J. D., Chung, I. J., Hill, K. G., and Battin-Pearson, S. (2001). "School and community risk factors and interventions. In Child Delinquents: Development, Intervention, and Service Needs," edited by R. Loeber and D. P. Farrington. Thousand Oaks, CA: Sage Publications, Inc., 211–246.

Heslop, L., and Enright, C. (2006). "Teens hurting teens." Ontario Victim Services Report. London, Ontario.

Hicks, K., and Hinck, S. (2009). "Best-practice intervention for care of clients who self mutilate." *Journal of the American Academy of Nurse Practitioners* 21(8), 430–436.

Institute for Children and Poverty. "Homelessness: The Foster Care Connection," (New York: Homes for the Homeless, 1993). National Coalition for the Homeless, "Breaking the Foster Care—Homelessness Connection," Sept./Oct. 1998. Web downloaded from www.nationalhomeless.org/sn/1998/sept/foster.html, however no longer available online.

Jubilee Action: "Bringing hope. Changing lives. (2002–2011). Available at www.jubileeaction.co.uk/resources.

Juvenile Fire starters (2003, February). "What you can do?" Federal Emergency Management Agency. [Brochure].

Kidd, S.A., et. al,. (2007, January) "Stories of working with homeless youth: On being 'mind-boggling.'" Children and Youth Services Review, 29(1), 16–34.

"Kids are waiting." Retrieved September 11, 2010. www.kidsarewaiting.org/assets/docs/PL%20110–351%20Summary.

Leone, P., Quinn, M., and Osher, D. (2002). "Collaboration in the juvenile justice system and youth serving agencies: Improving prevention, providing more efficient services, and reducing recidivism for youth with disabilities." Washington, DC: American Institutes for Research. Retrieved February 1, 2010. cecp.air.org/juvenilejustice/docs/Collaboration%20in%20the%20Juvenile%20Justice%20System.pdf.

Lipsey, M.W., and Derzon, J.H. (1998). "Predictors of violent and serious delinquency in adolescence and early adulthood: a synthesis of longitudinal research." In: Loeber, R., and Farrington, D. P., editors. Serious and violent juvenile offenders: risk factors and successful interventions. Thousand Oaks, CA: Sage Publications, 86–105.

Los Angeles Times, "Study of Runaway Youths Finds One-Third Were In Foster Care," as reported in *St. Louis Post-Dispatch* (January 19, 1992).

Lundman, R. J. (1993). *Prevention and Control of Delinquency.* 2d ed. New York: Oxford University Press.

Lyons-Ruth, K., and Jacobvitz, D. (1999). "Attachment disorganization: unresolved loss, relational violence and lapses in behavioral and attentional strategies." In J. Cassidy and P. Shaver (Eds.) Handbook of Attachment (520–554). Publisher: The Guilford Press; 1 edition (August 13, 1999) Language: English ISBN 1–57230–480–4ISBN 978–1-57230–480–82.

McCaffrey, E. (1994, April 13). "Caught in a Twilight Zone." *San Diego Union-Tribune.*

McMaster, N. (2009, October 13). "3 teens set another on fire, police say." www.newser.com/ story/71612/3-teens-set-another-on-fire-police-say.html.

Mercy, J., Butchart, A., Farrington, D., and Cerdá, M. "Youth violence." In: Krug, E., Dahlberg, L. L., Mercy, J., Zwi, A. B., and Lozano, R., editors (2002). "World report on violence and health". Geneva: World Health Organization, 25–56.

Mitchell, F. (2003, February). "Can I Come Home? The Experiences of Young Runaways Contacting the Message Home Helpline." Child and Family Social Work, 8(1), 3–11.

Morrison, B. (2002, February). "Bullying and victimisation in schools: A restorative justice approach." *Trends and Issues in Crime and Criminal Justice No. 219.* Canberra, Australia: Australian Institute of Criminology. Retrieved October 3, 2010. www.aic.gov.au/publications/tandi/ti219.pdf.

Mountain Homes Youth Ranch Program. www.mhyr.com/program/our-program-1.html.

National Association of Cognitive Behavioral Therapists (2009). Cognitive Behavioral Therapy. Retrieved on August 4, 2010. www.nacbt.org/whatiscbt.htm.

National Crime Prevention Council. Programs to Reduce Juvenile Violence. Retrieved October, 3 2010. www.ncpc.org/topics/school-safety/strategies/strategy-training-school-personnel-in-crime-prevention.

National Data Archive on Child Abuse and Neglect (2007). National Child Abuse and Neglect Data Systems. Retrieved July 28, 2010. www.ndacan.cornell.edu/index.html.

Office of National Drug Control Policy (2009). www.whitehousedrugpolicy.gov/about/foia.html.

O'Neil, S. (2008). "Bullying by tween and teen girls: A literature, policy, and resource review." Kookaburra Consulting, Inc.

"Problems of homeless youths: Empirical findings and human services issues" (1991, July). *Social Work* 36(4), 309–314.

Puzzanchera C. (2008). "Juvenile Justice Bulletin, Juvenile Arrests." Washington, DC: Office of Juvenile Justice and Delinquency Prevention 2009. Retrieved June 14, 2010. www.ncjrs.gov.

Puzzanchera, C. (2009). "Juvenile Arrests 2008".Washington, DC: U.S. Department of Justice, Office of Justice Programs, Office of Juvenile Justice and Delinquency Prevention.

Resnick, M. D., Ireland, M., and Borowsky, I. (2004). "Youth violence perpetration: what protects? What predicts?" Findings from the National Longitudinal Study of Adolescent Health. *Journal of Adolescent Health* 35(424), 1–10.

Raising the Roof (2008). "Homelessness in Canada the Road to Solutions." Retrieved July 2, 2010, from intraspec.ca/RoadtoSolutions_fullrept_english.pdf.

"Relational Aggression: More than Just Mean Girls." Retrieved on October 2, 2010. www.spsk12.net/departments/specialed/relational%20Aggression.htm.

Riley, D. B., et al. (2004, March–April). "Common themes and treatment approaches in working with families of runaway youths." *The American Journal of Family Therapy*, 32(2), 139–153.

Rosenback, M., et al. (2001). "State Children's Health Program." Retreived October 13, 2010. www.mathematica-mpr.com/pdfs/schip1.pdf.

Roman, N. P., and Wolfe, N. (1995). "Web of failure: The relationship between foster care and homelessness." Washington, DC: National Alliance to End Homelessness.

School Violence Legal Definition retrieved August 2, 2010. www. legal-dictionary .thefreedictionary.com/school+violence.

"School violence, weapons, crimes and bullying." Retrieved September 12, 2010. www.nssc1.org/.

"School Information System: School Climate Archives." Retrieved September 2, 2010. www.schoolinfosystem.org/archives/school_climate/index.php.

Shukula, P. C. (2005). *Street Children and the Asphalt Life: Delinquent Street Children*. India: ISHA Publisher.

Snyder, H. N. (2001). *Epidemiology of official offending. Child Delinquents: Development, Intervention, and Service Needs*. Edited by R. Loeber and D. P. Farrington. Thousand Oaks, CA: Sage Publications, Inc., 25–46.

Staller, K. M. (2004, July–September). "Runaway youth system dynamics: A theoretical framework for analyzing runaway and homeless youth policy." *Families in Society* 85(3), 379–390.

Stenhjem, P. (2005, February). "Youth with disabilities in the juvenile justice system: Prevention and intervention strategies." Examining Current Challenges in Secondary Education and Transition, 4(1).

"Street Children." Retrieved November 19, 2010. en.wikipedia.org/wiki/Street_Kids.

Street Connect. General intervention strategies. Retrieved November 21, 2010, from streetconnect.org/research/general-strategies.html.

Streib,V. L. (2000). "The juvenile death penalty today: Death sentences and executions for juvenile crimes," January 1, 1973–June 30, 2000. Ada, OH: Ohio Northern University, Claude W. Pettit College of Law.

Tarren-Sweeney, M., and Hazell, P. (2006, March). "Mental health of children in foster and kinship care in New South Wales, Australia." *Pediatric Child Health* 42(3), 89–97.

Testimony of Dennis Lepak. "Foster Care, Child Welfare, and Adoption Reforms." Joint Hearings before the Subcommittee on Public Assistance and Unemployment Compensation of the Committee on Ways and Means and the Select Committee on Children, Youth and Families, U.S. House of Representatives, April 13 and 28, May 12, 1988.

The Fostering Connections to Success and Increasing Adoptions Act of 2008 Kids Are Waiting Bill Summary for PL 110–351. Retrieved September 3, 2010, from www.kidsarewaiting.org/assets/docs/PL%20110–351%20Summary.

Thoma. R. (2010). "Foster Care Outcomes." Retrieved October 2010. www.liftingtheveil.org/foster14.htm.

Thompson, S. J., et al. (2004, December). "Runaway youth utilizing crisis shelter services: predictors of presenting problems." *Child and Youth Care Forum* 33(6), 387–404.

Thompson, S. J., et al. (2003, July). "Examining risk factors associated with family reunification for runaway youth: Does ethnicity matter?" *Family Relations* 52(3), 296–304.

Thompson, S. J., et al. (2001, September). "Differences and predictors if family reunification among subgroups of runaway youths using shelter services." *Social Work Research* 25(3), 163–172.

Umbreit, M. (2000). *Family group conferencing: Implications for crime victims.* St. Paul, MN: University of Minnesota, School of Social Work, Center for Restorative Justice and Peacemaking.

Umbreit, M., and Fercello, C. (1997). Interim report: Client evaluation of the victim/offender conferencing program in Washington County (MN). St. Paul, MN: University of Minnesota, School of Social Work, Center for Restorative Justice and Peacemaking.

UNICEF. "Child trafficking." Retrieved December 26, 2010. www.unicef.org/ protection/index_exploitation.html.

UNICEF. (2006, January 25). "Ethiopia: Steady increase in street children orphaned by AIDS." Available from www.unicef.org/infobycountry/ethiopia_30783.html.

U.S. Department of Commerce, Bureau of the Census, July 1, 2008. Estimates of the Resident Population by Selected Age Groups for the United States and Puerto Rico.

Veeran, V. (2004, October)."Working with street children: A child-centered Approach." *Child Care in Practice* 10(4), 59–366.

"Violence and Weapons." Everyday Law Encyclopedia. Retrieved September 12, 2010. www.enotes.com/everyday-law-encyclopedia/violence-and-weapons.

V. Roman, N. P., and Wolfe, N. (1995). *Web of failure: The relationship between foster care and homelessness.* Washington, DC: National Alliance to End Homelessness.

"Which Way is Home?" yourbloodismyblood.blogspot.com. Retrieved September 4, 2010.

Wikipedia. "Foster Care." Retrieved August 8, 2010. en.wikipedia.org/wiki/Foster_care.

About the Author

Marcel Lebrun has been an educator for 32 years. During that time he has been a classroom teacher, administrator, school counselor, and special education teacher. He is presently a professor and Chair at Plymouth State University in the Department of Education. He teaches classes in special education, behavior management, counseling, and educational methodology at the undergraduate and graduate level. He has taught abroad and traveled extensively throughout the world. Lebrun has published several books on depression, sexual orientation, school shootings, keeping kids safe and healthy, as well as several articles on behavior issues and mental health concerns in children. Lebrun works mostly with school personnel around student issues in violence, aggression, functional assessment, and mental health concerns. Dr. Lebrun was honored with Distinguished Professor of the Year for 2008.